Recipes
From Missouri
With Love

by
Sandy Buege

Special Thanks
Special thanks to Jo Roche and Barbara Daniel who typed the manuscript and made sense out of my notes and some old recipes. To all my friends at work who encouraged me and contributed recipes and to neighbors, who through the years shared their best recipes with me.

ISBN: 0-913703-13-3
1st PRINTING: SEPTEMBER 1986
2nd PRINTING: JULY 1990
3rd PRINTING: DECEMBER 1993
Copyright © 1986 by Sandy Buege

Published by The Branches, Inc.
          1389 Park Road
          Chanhassen, MN 53617

Ordering information for additional copies is located at the back of the book.

Dedication

To good cooks everywhere.

To the women in my family who love to cook and the men who appreciate their efforts.

Most of all to my mother, whose patience allowed me to mess up her kitchen when I was just "knee high to a grasshopper" and learning to cook.

Quilt Designs

Each chapter is bordered by a different Missouri Heritage Quilt Design, which is described and identified at the beginning of each chapter. These lovely antique designs are a pictorial glimpse into Missouri's diverse history and lore.

Contents

SAMPLE MENUS

Let's Get Together Party Menu
Steamboat Spinach Balls
Sauerkraut Balls
Balloon Race Mostaciolli
Party Cheese Ball
Assorted Crackers and Rolls
Ham Roll-Ups
Homemade Peach Ice Cream
Grandma's Butter Crisps

Menu for a Cold Winter Night's Supper
Hot Apple Cider
Wilted Lettuce Salad
Hearty Short Ribs
Oven Browned Potatoes
Carrots
Sourdough Bread
French Chocolate Silk Pie

Menu for a Celebration Dinner
Dry White Missouri Wine
Spinach Salad
Chicken Asparagus Casserole
Spooky Wild Rice
Green Bean Amandine
Celebration Cheesecake
Espresso

Menu for a Sunday Brunch
Mimosa's and Bloody Marys
Broiled Grapefruit
Swiss Eggs
Blueberry Muffins
Bran Muffins
Sweet Kewpie Compote
Prize Winning Coffee Cake
Hot Coffee and Tea
Hot Chocolate

Menu for a Fourth of July Picnic
Orange Lemonade
Cold Southern Fried Chicken
Potato Salad
Bean Medley
Fresh Vegetable Salad
Cracklin Corn Bread
Carrot Sticks and Celery Sticks
with Dill Dip
Strawberry Shortcake

MISSOURI HERITAGE QUILT DESIGN — **PINEBURR**
MAKER: JOELLA GRAVES CARPENTER 1858–1938
This scrap quilt of Missouri contains fabric spanning 40–45 years, including imported prints and **art noveau** designs.

Appetizers and Party Foods

SAUERKRAUT BALLS

2 tbsp. shortening
½ cup finely chopped onion
½ cup chopped ham
½ cup chopped corn beef
¼ tsp. seasoned salt
1 cup well drained finely chopped sauerkraut
3 tbsp. milk
2 eggs, beaten
⅓ cup flour
⅓ cup stock or bouillon
¼ cup flour
  fine dry breadcrumbs

Melt butter, add onion and cook over medium heat for 5 minutes. Add ham, corned beef and sauerkraut. Cook 5 minutes stirring occasionally.

Blend in ⅓ cup flour, gradually add stock or bouillon, salt and mix well.

Chill and shape into 1" balls.

Blend ¼ cup flour with milk, add eggs and mix.

Dip kraut balls in egg mixture and coat with bread crumbs.

Fry in deep fat at 375 for 2–3 minutes. Drain on paper towels.

Serve with toothpicks.

Ancient winds blew east across America depositing clouds of dust from the Northwest corner of Missouri to the Dakotas. Over a thousand years this dust was piled layer upon layer forming mounds up to 200 feet thick. This strange yellow dirt is called loess. It is only found in China and a very few other places. If you drive Highway 1-29 you can drive through walls of this strange earth.

HOT CHILI DIP

1 can chili (without beans)
1 cup Velveeta cheese, cut up
1 4 oz. can green chili peppers, chopped
2 tbsp. minced onion

Mix all together and bake for 1 hour at 275°.
Serve with Doritos or Tortilla cheese crackers.

During the war with Mexico, Col. Alexander Doniphan led a small regiment of 1,000 Missouri volunteers. These brave men traveled some 3,000 miles and survived cold, hunger and the enemy with a loss of only 50 men.

STEAMBOAT SPINACH BALLS

2 boxes chopped spinach
2 cups herb stuffing mix
2 onions, chopped
¾ cup butter
½ cup Parmesan cheese
⅔ tsp thyme
½ tsp. pepper
1 tsp. M.S.G.
1 tbsp. garlic salt

Cook spinach and drain well. Add other ingredients.

Put in refrigerator for about 1 hour until workable. Shape into large marble-size balls.

Bake at 350° for 20 minutes.

You can still ride on a steamboat on the Mississippi today. The Delta Queen and the Mississippi Queen transport guests in luxurious comfort down the Mississippi.

PARTY CHEESE BALL
"Make Ahead for a Party"

1 package (8 oz.) cream cheese
½ lb. (or less) Bleu cheese, crumbled
¼ lb. sharp cheddar cheese, grated
1 small onion, grated or minced
1 tbsp. worcestershire sauce
1 tbsp. lemon juice
½ cup chopped pecans
finely chopped parsley

Place all ingredients except pecans and parsley in mixer bowl. Let stand at room temperature until softened.

Mix well on medium speed. Stir in pecans.

Spread parsley on waxed paper. Turn cheese mixture onto parsley and fold paper up around sides, shaping mixture into a ball.

Parsley will cling to surface of ball.

Chill 3 or 4 hours. Provide cheese spreader.

In 1856, two brothers opened a distillery in Weston, Missouri. The cold limestone spring water made a fine bourbon. The Holladay Distillery is known today as the McCormick Distillery and is America's oldest continuously operating distillery.

CRAB, CREAM CHEESE AND CHILI SAUCE

8 oz. cream cheese
1 package frozen crab meat,
thawed, cooked and drained

Soften cream cheese and spread on serving platter. Cover with crabmeat. Just before serving top with chili sauce mixture. Serve with assorted crackers.

Sauce:

½ cup chili sauce
1 tsp. horseradish
1 tsp. worcestershire sauce
¼ tsp tabasco
2 tbsp. lemon juice
1 tsp chopped chives
¼ tsp. parsley
1 tsp salt

To categorize Missouri as a northern state, a southern state, or even a midwestern state would not be entirely accurate. It belongs to all of these regions and more; it truly is the heartland of America, filled with much of the nation's wonderful diversity.

BUFFALO MOZZARELLA STICKS

2¼ lbs. mozzarella cheese
½ cup vinegar
2 tsp. tomato paste
1 tsp. Louisiana hot sauce
½ tsp. garlic powder
    pepper
¾ cup flour
2 eggs, beaten
1½ cup breadcrumbs

Cut cheese into small sticks.

Marinate cheese sticks in the vinegar, tomato paste, hot red pepper sauce, garlic powder and pepper for 8 hours.

Remove cheese from marinade.

Roll in flour, then egg, then breadcrumbs.

Refrigerate until chilled.

Deep fry at 350 until golden, about 1 to 2 minutes. Drain on paper towels.

Serve immediately.

George Caleb Bingham's house in Arrow Rock has been carefully preserved. This famous American artist first began his sketches of Missouri boatmen, politicians and farmers from the real-life people he associated with in the area.

PICKLED EGGS

1 can (1 lb.) small whole beets, do not drain
1 cup cider vinegar
⅓ cup sugar
3 whole cloves
¾ tsp. salt
¼ cup water
8 hard cooked eggs, shelled

Empty beets and their liquid into a small saucepan. Add vinegar, sugar, salt and cloves. Heat just until sugar dissolves. Cool to room temperature.

Place eggs in a medium sized bowl or jar. Pour in the beet mixture and add just enough water so liquid covers eggs.

Cover and marinate in the refrigerator 2 to 3 days stirring now and then or inverting the jar several times so eggs will redden evenly.

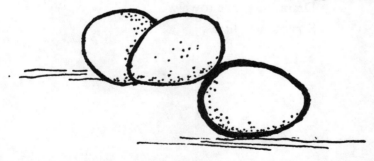

Jesse James is a legend in Missouri. He was called the Robin Hood of the 1870's. Jesse, along with the rest of the James Younger gang were all ex-Civil War guerrillas. Many people in Missouri sympathized with the gang. Robbing banks and railroads was one way of getting even with the Union. It was an era of lawlessness in Missouri.

CHECKERBOARD SQUARE PARTY MIX
(a favorite for years)

½ cup butter
1¼ tsp. seasoned salt
4½ tsp. worcestershire sauce
2⅔ cups Corn Chex cereal
2⅔ cups Rice Chex cereal
2⅔ cups Wheat Chex cereal
1 cup salted mixed nuts
2 cups pretzel sticks

Preheat oven to 250°.

Melt butter in large shallow pan. Remove from heat and stir in seasoned salt and worcestershire sauce.

Gradually add cereal, nuts and pretzels, mixing until all pieces are coated.

Bake 1 hour. Stir every 15 minutes.

Spread on paper towels to cool.

Makes 9 cups.

Ralston Purina has long been known to cat and dog owners. It not only makes food for animals, but people as well. Located in downtown St. Louis on Checkerboard Square, the name "Purina" came from the slogan "Where purity is paramount". We think you'll enjoy this party mix made with Ralston Purina products.

FOXY CHEESE BLINTZES

2 eggs	Beat together eggs, oil and milk. **Add flour and salt and beat until smooth.**
2 tbsp. salad oil	
1 cup milk	
¾ cup sifted flour	Chill ½ hour until batter is the consistency of heavy cream.
½ tsp. salt	
6 tbsp. butter	Melt 1 tbsp. butter in small frying pan. Pour 1 tbsp. of batter into pan turning pan so batter covers the bottom. Fry until lightly brown on one side only. Stack blintzes and fry rest of batter.

Filling:

6 oz. cream cheese	Beat all ingredients until smooth.
6 oz. cottage cheese	Place large tbsp. of cheese filling on each blintz. Fold over the two sides and roll up.
2 egg yolks	
2 tbsp. sugar	Fry filled blintzes in skillet until lightly browned.
1 tsp. vanilla extract	Serve hot with sour cream and a sprinkling of sugar.

They call her the "Fabulous Fox" of St. Louis. This grand old movie theatre of the 1920's has been lovingly restored to her Byzantine splendor and now hosts some of the nations best live entertainment. Try making some of these wonderful cheese blintzes for an after theatre supper.

FAVORITE RYE BREAD DIP

⅔ cup sour cream
⅔ cup mayonnaise
1 tsp. Beau Monde Seasoning
1 tsp. dill weed
1 tbsp. dried onion flakes
1 tbsp. finely chopped fresh
parsley

Mix all ingredients and let stand about 3 hours before serving. Using a large round loaf of rye bread, slice off the top of loaf and scoop out center. Cut bread into cubes, fill cavity with dip and place cubes around the loaf.

Double recipe for more than 6–8 people.

DILL

What little boy doesn't love a train, or big boys either, for that matter? The National Museum of Transport in St. Louis showcases a 150 year history of the railroads. Engines dating from pre-Civil War days can be seen along with more powerful recent models.

TOASTED RAVIOLI
(This is a recipe which is very St. Louis)

½ cup milk
2 eggs, beaten
2½ doz. frozen raviolis
¾ cup seasoned bread crumbs
    oil
    fresh grated parmesan
    cheese

Mix milk and eggs. Dip frozen ravioli into egg/milk mixture and then in bread crumbs.

Deep fry in oil heated to 350° until golden brown and rise to the top or about 3 to 4 minutes.

Remove from oil, drain on paper towels. Sprinkle generously with cheese.

Serve with a tomato meat sauce such as on page 90

Come to St. Louis over the 4th of July and be part of one of our nation's largest Birthday Celebrations. The Veiled Prophet Fair, started in 1878 by civic-minded businessmen celebrates the mysterious Veiled Prophet of Khorassan and his court. There is a parade, fireworks, food and some terrific entertainment.

PONY EXPRESS BEEF JERKY

1 lb. top round steak
½ cup soy sauce
1 tsp. worcestershire sauce
1 tsp. salt or garlic salt
black pepper

Chill meat in freezer for 1 to 2 hours. Cut meat across grain into ¼" strips. Put in shallow baking dish with other ingredients and refrigerate overnight.

Drain meat and dry on paper toweling. Bake in very slow oven, 250° for 4 hours or until dry and chewey but not crisp. A lower temperature of 150° for 8–10 hours is even better. Cool & refrigerate until used.

The Pony Express played a vital part in saving the West for the Union during the Civil War. The 400 daring men and boys braved hardships and danger to deliver the U.S. mail. They began their 2000 mile journey in St. Joseph, Mo., with Sacramento California as their destination. The development of the telegraph quickly put an end to this means of mail delivery but not before stories and legends of the men's bravery were handed down from generation to generation. They were always pressed for time so they often took some beef jerky with them on their long and tiring trip.

PICKLED MUSHROOMS

1 lb. fresh mushrooms
½ cup water
½ cup vinegar

1 cup white vinegar
1 tbsp. sugar
1 tsp. salt
1 shredded bay leaf
3 cloves
3 whole black peppers
2 cloves garlic, minced
1 sliced lemon

Clean and trim mushrooms. Boil mushrooms in a mixture of ½ cup water and ½ cup vinegar. Let boil for 3 minutes, drain and save liquid. Let cool.

Combine vinegar, seasonings and mushroom liquid. Boil 3–4 minutes and add mushrooms. Put into jar and let stand overnight or longer.

Missouri has over 6,000 caves. Some were found and used by early settlers. Indians used the caves as shelters, but in modern times they were used to house cattle. Some caves have been used as wine cellars but during prohibition, this stopped and the caves were then used to grow mushrooms.

HAM ROLLUPS

2–8 oz. pkg. cream cheese
3– pkgs. thinly sliced ham (12 oz.)
1 to 2 tsp. grated onion
⅛ tsp. dry mustard

Mix cheese, onion and mustard. Spread on ham slices. Roll up. Refrigerate 24 hours. Cut into 2 in. lengths.

Variation of above recipe. Spread ham slices with seasoned cream cheese. Place large dill pickle on one end and roll up. Refrigerate same as above.

BANDSTAND SUMMER SAUSAGE

2 lbs. ground chuck
¾ cup water
1 tbsp. liquid smoke
⅛ tsp. garlic powder
2 tbsp. Mortons quick cure
1 tbsp. mustard seed
¼ tsp. pepper
¼ tsp. salt
1 tbsp pepper corns

Mix together, mold into 2 long rolls. Wrap tightly in foil. Let stand in refrigerator 24 hours. Slit bottom of foil. Bake on rack in pan for 1 hour at 350° degrees. Let cool and chill.

The town square in Bethel, Mo. is neatly kept. The bandstand sits behind a white picket fence waiting for the band. Some of the band members have played for 50 years. Bethels band has played music for 142 years, entertaining the townspeople.

MISSOURI HERITAGE QUILT DESIGN — **COCKSCOMB AND CURRANTS**
MAKER: SUSAN A. SHIFLETT THORNE SMITH 1851–1941

This Missouri quilt was made by the bride as a wedding present in 1871. It is unique in its wonderful details. Imagine today a wedding present from your spouse worked on for years before the great day!

Breads and Breakfasts

CHOCOLATE-ALMOND ZUCCHINI BREAD

3 cups sifted flour
2 cups sugar
1¼ tsp. baking soda
1 tsp salt
1 tsp ground cinnamon
1 cup chopped blanched almonds
1 cup vegetable oil
1 tsp. vanilla
3 eggs
2 (1 oz.) sq. unsweetened chocolate, melted
2 cups shredded zucchini

Into a large bowl, sift together the first 6 ingredients. Stir in almonds.

In medium bowl, mix oil, vanilla, and eggs until well blended. Stir in melted chocolate until mixed well. Stir in zucchini.

Stir zucchini mixture into dry ingredients just until moistened. Pour batter into greased 9"x5"x3" loaf pan.

Bake 350° oven for 1 hour and 30 minutes or until toothpick inserted in center comes out clean.

Cool in pan 10 minutes. Remove, cool on rack.

Makes 1 large loaf.

There are over 160 species of trees in Missouri, more than 2,000 species of plants and 700 mammals, birds and reptiles.

WAGON TRAIN SOURDOUGH BREAD

Starters: There are basically two ways to get a sourdough starter.

Method 1:

   1 cup milk
   1 cup flour

Place milk in glass or crock and allow to stand 24 hours.

Stir in flour, cover with cheesecloth and place outside for several hours to expose to wild yeast cells floating in the wind.

Leave uncovered for 2 to 5 days until mixture begins to bubble and sour. (If it begins to dry add enough water so original consistency is maintained).

Starter is best if used at least once a week. If not used for 2 to 3 weeks, remove half the starter and replenish with fresh starter. Starter can be frozen but should be allowed to stand at room temperature for 24 hours before using.

Each time the starter is used, replenish it with equal parts milk and flour allowing to stand several hours to get bubbly. Cover and store in the refrigerator.

Method 2:

   1 cake or package yeast dissolved in
   2 cups warm water
   Add 2 cups flour

Place in glass or crockery bowl and let stand 3 to 4 days.

When mixture begins to ferment, skim off top. Add enough flour and water to make a paste consistency.

SOURDOUGH BREAD

1½ cups warm water
1 package yeast
1 cup sourdough starter
4 cups unsifted flour
2 tsp. sugar
2 tsp. salt
½ tsp. soda
2 cups unsifted flour

Pour warm water into bowl and dissolve yeast. Add starter, 4 cups of flour, salt and sugar. Stir vigorously for about 3 minutes. Turn into a large greased bowl. Cover with clean towel and let rise until double (about 1½ to 2 hours).

Mix soda with 1 cup of remaining flour and stir in.

Turn dough onto floured board and begin kneading. Add remaining flour to control stickiness. Knead until satiny and smooth (about 8 minutes).

Shape into 2 loaves or 1 large round loaf. Cover and place in a warm area. Let rise until double in bulk (about 1½ hours).

Before baking brush tops of loaves with water and make diagonal cuts with a sharp knife.

Bake on a greased cookie sheet in a hot oven (400°) for 45–50 minutes.

Place a pan of hot water in bottom of oven while baking bread.

Independence, Missouri and the bustling town of Westport, became major outfitting points for every Western settler traveling either the Santa Fe or the Oregon Trails. The call "Wagons Ho" could be heard daily. Early women were hardpressed to provide palatable food for their families. Sourdough bread was one way to fill stomachs, and is still popular today.

CRACKLIN' CORN BREAD

4 oz. **finely diced pork fat (1 cup)**
   1 **cup cornmeal**
   1 **cup all purpose flour**
   1 **tsp. baking soda**
  ¾ **tsp. salt**
   1 **cup buttermilk**
   2 **beaten eggs**

Fry pork fat until crisp. Drain, reserving ⅓ cup of drippings. In large bowl mix together cornmeal, flour, baking soda and salt. Add buttermilk, eggs and drippings. Beat until smooth. Stir in cracklings. Bake in a greased 10" skillet at 425° until done (about 15–20 minutes). Serve warm. Makes 6 servings.

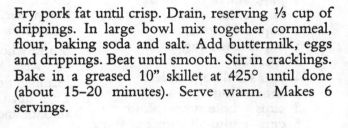

Mark Twain, Hannibal's most famous person immortalized the feeling of small town life on the Mississippi. If you visit Hannibal today, you can almost be transported back in time and think that at any moment you might see Tom Sawyer and Huck Finn with their fishing poles, walking barefoot down to the river. Tom always had a piece of cracklin bread and some cold fried chicken to share with Huck.

WHOLE WHEAT BREAD
The Midwest's Most Popular Choice

1 pkg. active dry yeast
¼ cup water
2½ cups hot water
½ cup brown sugar
3 tsp. salt
¼ cup solid vegetable
shortening
3 cups whole wheat flour
5 cups white all-purpose flour

Soften dry yeast in ¼ cup warm water. Combine hot water, sugar, salt and shortening; cool to lukewarm.

Stir in whole wheat flour and 1 cup of white flour. Stir well. Mix in softened yeast. Add enough remaining flour to make a moderately stiff dough. Turn out on a lightly floured surface. Knead until smooth and satiny—10 to 12 minutes.

Shape dough into a ball. Place in a lightly greased bowl, turning over to grease surface. Cover and let rise in warm place until double in size (about 1½ hour). Punch down. Cut in 2 portions. Shape each in smooth ball. Cover with clean cloth and let rest 10 minutes.

Shape into loaves; place in greased 8½x4½x2½" loaf pans. Let rise until double, about 1¼ hours.

Bake in moderate oven, 375° for 45 minutes. If softer crust is desired, cover with foil last 20 minutes. Makes 2 loaves.

Kansas City is one of the world's great agri-business capitals. The Board of Trade, a commodities exchange center is open each weekday, where the world's largest winter wheat market is in session. It is an exciting place to visit when trading is heavy in the "pit".

PAPAW BREAD

Mix together:

1¾ cups all purpose flour
2¼ tsp. baking powder
½ tsp. salt

Blend until creamy:

⅓ cup shortening
⅔ cup sugar
¾ tsp. lemon rind, grated

Beat in:

2 eggs, beaten
1¼ cups ripe papaw

Fold in:

½ cup coarsely chopped walnuts
¼ cup finely chopped apricots

Add the sifted ingredients in about 3 parts to the sugar mixture. Beat after each addition until smooth.

Place the batter in greased and floured loaf pan. Bake at 350° for 1 hour or until done. Cool before slicing.

Papaw is a fruit which grows in Missouri and ripens in the fall. It has a knobby green skin and when peeled, tastes much like a lemony banana.

The town of Branson, Missouri inspired author Harold Bell Wright in 1907 to write *The Shepherd of the Hills*, a novel which became the fourth best seller of all times. It tells of the simple dignity of the people of the Ozarks and a sad and mysterious tale. The story is reenacted at the Shepherd of the Hills Farm in performances from May to October.

SPOONBREAD

1 cup yellow or white
  cornmeal
1 tsp. salt
3 cups milk, scalded
2 tbsp. butter
2 tsp. baking powder
4 eggs, separated

Heat milk in saucepan or double boiler. Combine cornmeal with milk and mix. Add egg yolks and cook until thick and mixture is the consistency of mush. Remove from heat, add butter, baking powder and salt.

Beat egg whites until stiff and fold into cornmeal mixture.

Spoon into buttered 2 qt. casserole. Bake uncovered at 375° for 40 to 50 minutes, until golden brown and puffy (or until knife inserted in center comes out clean). Makes 8 servings.

Couples get married in unusual places. They say that the first couple to be married in Bridal Cave was an Osage Indian warrior and maiden. Since that time, almost 1,000 couples have been married in the cave in Thunder Mountain Park, near Camdenton, Missouri.

LOVER'S LEAP POPPY SEED BREAD

3 cups flour
1½ tsp. poppy seed
1½ tsp. salt
1½ tsp. baking powder
2⅓ cups sugar
1½ tsp. vanilla
1½ tsp. butter flavoring
1½ tsp. almond flavoring
3 eggs
1½ cups milk
1⅓ cups cooking oil

Mix dry ingredients well, then add remaining ingredients, mix thoroughly. Bake in greased loaf pans at 375° for 1 hour and 10 minutes. (if using small loaf pan, bake 40–45 minutes) Test for doneness. Let cool 5 min, remove from pan and glaze.

The high bluffs along the Mississippi near Hannibal tell their own story. They say that two young men in love with the beautiful young daughter of a coon hunter made a bet that whoever could race (on foot) to a spot near the edge of the cliff and get there first would have the hand of the young lady. The loser would have to keep on running right over the edge. It turned out to be a tie—the sensible young men shook hands and walked away. The beautiful girl was so disgusted that she ran off and married a fisherman. Before she left town though, she made her daddy a loaf of poppy seed bread.

PRAIRIE PUMPKIN BREAD

3⅓ cups flour
2 tsp. baking soda
1½ tsp. salt
1 tsp. cinnamon
1 tsp. nutmeg
1 tsp. cloves (opt.)
1 cup corn oil
4 eggs
4 tsp. water
2 cups pumpkin
3 cups sugar
1 cup nuts (opt.)

Mix all ingredients together, grease three loaf pans and divide batter evenly. Bake at 350° for 1 hour.

Laura Ingalls Wilder wrote her famous stories at her farm in Mansfield, where she and Almonzo moved from the Dakotas. She lived to be 90 years old and always baked her favorite pumpkin bread whenever her children and grandchildren came to visit.

MOLLY'S STRAWBERRY BREAD

3 cups all purpose flour
1 tsp. baking soda
1 tsp. salt
1½ tsp. cinnamon
2 cups sugar
2 10 oz. pkgs. frozen (thawed) sliced strawberries
4 beaten eggs
1¼ cup oil
1 cup chopped pecans

Sift together dry ingredients. Place sifted ingredients in a large bowl and make a well in center. Place strawberries (with juice), eggs, oil, and pecans in well and stir until ingredients are moistened. Bake in a greased and floured loaf pans. Bake at 350° for 1 hour and 15 minutes. Test after 1 hour. Cool in pan 30 minutes before turning onto rack. Bread freezes well. Good served with butter or strawberry jam.

Makes 2 large loaves or 3 small loaves

Molly Brown, that lovable tenacious woman from the Broadway play and movie, "The Unsinkable Molly Brown", was born in Hannibal, Mo., in a two room frame house on the edge of town. She never forgot how to treat people, no matter how rich she became, and her hospitality is echoed in Missouri homes across the state. It is said that she had a loaf of strawberry bread with her on board the Titanic, and that it fed everyone in her lifeboat for a full week. We don't know if that's true or not, but here's the recipe for Molly's Strawberry Bread.

OLD FASHIONED
FUZZY DUCK NUT BREAD

1½ cups walnuts
3 cups sifted flour
1 cup sugar
4 tsp. baking powder
1½ tsp. salt
1 egg (beat lightly)
¼ cup melted shortening
1½ cup milk
1 tsp. vanilla

Coarsely chop walnuts, Resift flour with sugar, baking powder and salt. Add egg, shortening, milk and vanilla to dry mixture. Stir just until all the flour is moistened. Stir in walnuts.

Turn into greased 9 x 5 x 3" loaf pan. Bake at 350° for 1 hour and 20 min.

Swan Lake National Wildlife Refuge was established during the dustbowl years of the depression. Congress feared for the future of migratory waterfowl life. The refuge was originally supposed to provide a habitat for prairie chickens and ducks, but soon geese found it attractive as well.

Over 100,000 Canada Geese are here every year along with 200 other species of birds, including about 100 bald eagles. The refuge is near Sumner, Missouri, and is open to the public.

OATMEAL BREAD

Combine in large bowl:

- 1 cup Quick Oatmeal
- 1 tbsp. salt
- ⅓ cup shortening
- ½ cup molasses or ¼ cup molasses plus ¼ cup honey

Pour over this, 1½ cups boiling water and cool to lukewarm.

Add:

- 2 cups flour (beat well)
- 2 eggs (beaten)
- 1 cake or pkg. yeast (soften in ½ cup water)

Knead and put in a large bowl. Let rise until doubled in size. Punch down and form into loaves. This makes either 3 small loaves or 2 large loaves. Let the dough rise again until the tops reach the edges of the pan. Bake at 325° for 45 minutes to 1 hour.

oats

Calloway County was settled before the Civil War, by Southerners from Virginia, Kentucky and Tennessee. It is a belt across the center of the state and was known as "Little Dixie". The settlers brought with them their Southern traditions and some fine thoroughbred horses. We know that mares eat oats, but we think that you'll enjoy this recipe for Oatmeal Bread.

LITTLE BOY BLUEBERRY ORANGE BREAD

2 tbsp. butter
¼ cup boiling water
3 tsp. grated orange rind
½ cup orange juice
1 egg
1 cup sugar
2 cups sifted flour
1 tsp. baking powder
¼ tsp. soda
½ tsp. salt
2 tbsp. honey
1 cup fresh or frozen blueberries

Melt butter in boiling water in small bowl. Add juice, and rind. Beat eggs with sugar until light and fluffy. Add dry ingredients alternately with orange liquid, beating until smooth. Fold in berries. Bake in greased 9x5x3 pan at 325° for 1 hour and 10 minutes. Turn out onto rack. Mix 2 tbsp. orange juice, 1 tsp. rind and 2 tbsp. honey. Spoon over hot loaf. Let stand until cool.

Eugene Field, the beloved and well known children's poet, was born in St. Louis in 1850. His boyhood home is now a museum filled with antique toys and visited by thousands of school children every year. His most famous poem is one that all children learn—"Little Boy Blue". Schools all over the country are named for this author who was also an accomplished journalist. This recipe for blueberry orange bread is sure to be a favorite with kids and grownups alike!

ORANGE GLAZE

1½ tsp. butter flavoring
1½ tsp. almond flavoring
1½ tsp. vanilla flavoring
 ¼ cup orange juice
 ⅓ cup sugar

Mix ingredients and use as glaze on warm bread.

THE NEW MISSOURI MIX

8   cups flour
¼   cup baking powder plus 1 tbsp.
2   tsp. salt
1   cup nonfat dry milk powder
1½ cups solid vegetable shortening

Combine dry ingredients in a large bowl. Sift ingredients to assure even distribution. Using a large fork or pastry blender, cut in shortening until mix is the consistency of cornmeal.

Makes 11 cups. Store in an airtight container. May be frozen or refrigerated.

Missouri Mix can be used in any recipe calling for commercial baking mix or in your favorite recipes. Simply substitute mix for flour using 1½ cups mix for each cup of flour in your recipe. Leave out leavening, salt, milk and fat in your recipe, because they are already in the Mix.

BASIC BLUEBERRY MUFFINS

2 cups Missouri Mix
2 tbsp. sugar
1 egg, beaten
1 cup water
½ cup fresh, frozen or canned
& drained blueberries

Stir sugar into Mix. Beat egg and add to the water. Add liquid to dry ingredients and stir 15 strokes, or just enough to blend, leaving a few lumps. Bake in a well greased muffin tin at 400° for 20 minutes. Makes 10 to 12 medium muffins.

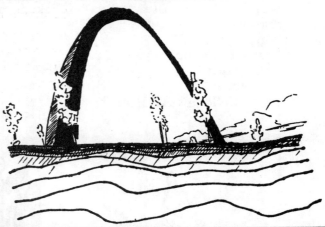

The Gateway Arch in St. Louis, designed by Eero Saarinen, is the nations tallest monument. Symbolizing the opening of the West, the Arch is the fourth most visited man-made monument in the world. Completion of the Arch and the Museum of Westward Expansion beneath it took 15 years. Its silver beauty is especially lovely at night with the mighty Mississippi rippling in the moonlight nearby.

BRAN MUFFINS

2 cups boiling water
2 cups Nabisco 100% bran
1 cup good quality solid
  vegetable shortening
  (heaping)
3 cups sugar
2 tsp. salt
4 eggs
1 quart buttermilk
5 cups flour
5 tsp. soda
4 cups Kellogg's All Bran

Pour boiling water over Nabisco Bran and let cool. Cream shortening, sugar, eggs, milk and cooled bran. Sift flour, soda, salt and add to the above. This mix can be kept in a closed container for one month in the refrigerator.
Bake in muffin tins at 350° for 20 minutes.

SPEEDY BISCUITS

2 cups all-purpose flour
3 tsp. baking powder
½ tsp. salt
½ cup shortening
¾ cup milk

In a mixing bowl, thoroughly stir together flour, baking powder, and salt. Cut in shortening with a pastry blender or blend with a fork till mixture resembles coarse crumbs. Make a well in the center of the dry mixture; add milk all at once. Stir with a fork just till the dough clings together and follows the fork around the bowl. Turn the dough out onto a lightly floured surface; knead it gently 10 to 12 strokes. Roll or pat the dough to ½ inch thickness. Cut the dought with a floured 2½ inch biscuit cutter, rerolling as needed. Place on an ungreased baking sheet; bake in 450 degree oven for 12 minutes or till biscuits are golden. Serve warm. Makes 8 biscuits.

In 1902, men raced a new-fangled contraption called an automobile. They ran over pigs, chickens and various other wildlife, resulting in the county passing a speed limit of 8 miles per hour. In 1903, this was raised to 9 miles per hour and an annual fee of $2.00 was placed on each automobile for the purpose of upgrading county roads. Women had to keep up with this preoccupation with speed and often whipped together these speedy biscuits for dinner!

FLAVORED BUTTERS

Orange Butter
- ½ lb. butter
- ¼ cup orange juice
  grated rind of 1 orange

Strawberry Butter
- ½ lb. butter
- ¼ cup strawberry preserves

Honey Butter
- ½ lb. butter
- ½ cup honey

Spice Butter
- ½ lb. butter
- ½ tsp. cinnamon
- ½ tsp. nutmeg

Whip butter with flavorings until fluffy. Adjust and add more flavorings if desired.

These butters are very good with biscuits and fruit breads.

The American Royal Livestock Horse Show and Rodeo held every year in Kansas City since 1899, is one of the most outstanding events of its kinds. Because it draws competitors from 35 states and Canada it is considered the foremost livestock show in America today.

PRIZE WINNING COFFEE CAKE

2 cups flour
1½ cups sugar
¼ cup butter
¼ cup shortening or margarine
3 tsp. baking powder
¾ tsp. salt
3 eggs, separated
¾ cup milk

Sift together flour, sugar, baking powder and salt. Cut together with butter and shortening until well mixed. Reserve one cup of the mixture.

To remainder, add beaten egg yolks and milk, fold in whites. Pour batter into 8"x12" pan, which has been greased on the bottom. Sprinkle reserved mixture on top.

NOTE: you can add finely grated almonds, cinnamon or coconut to the top, if you wish.

Bake 35 minutes in 350° oven.

Joseph Pulitzer, a young Hungarian immigrant to Missouri, was a crusading journalist who fought corruption and vice in any form. He bought a bankrupt paper, the St. Louis Post and was offered a merger with the successful St. Louis Dispatch. Today the Post Dispatch is still printing the news for Missourians and the nationally known Pulitzer Prize for journalism excellence honors his name.

RAILROAD FRENCH TOAST
(Remember the dining cars of day's gone past?)

10 slices bread
    soft butter
¾ cup brown sugar
1 tsp. cinnamon
1½ cups flour
1¼ tsp. baking powder
½ tsp. salt
2 eggs, separated
1 cup milk
3 tbsp. melted butter

Spread bread with butter. Sprinkle half the bread with brown sugar into which the cinnamon has been mixed. Cover slices with remaining slices, making sandwiches. Cut sandwiches into quarters. Mix together flour, baking powder and salt. Add egg yolks, milk and melted butter. Mix well. Beat egg whites until stiff and fold into batter. Dip each sandwich into batter, coating well. Fry in ½" of oil and butter in hot skillet until brown, turning once. Sprinkle with confectioner's sugar and serve with jelly.

Union Station in St. Louis first opened its doors in 1894. Through the years 1904 to the 1940s, Union Station was the busiest, biggest passenger rail terminal in the world, handling up to 100,000 passengers a day. After the advent of air travel, Union Station fell onto hard times. Designated as a National Historic Landmark in 1978, its recent renovation is the largest commercial project of National Historic Landmarks in America.

FLOAT TRIP HUSH PUPPIES
(Serve these around the campfire with the fish you caught)

¼ tsp. baking soda
½ cup buttermilk
1 cup cornmeal
½ tsp. baking powder
½ tsp. salt
1 egg, beaten
¼ cup finely chopped onion
vegetable oil for frying

Dissolve soda in buttermilk, stir well. Combine cornmeal, baking powder and salt. Stir in buttermilk mixture, egg and onion, mixing well.

Drop batter by tablespoonfuls into deep hot oil (350°). Fry about 3 minutes per side or until golden brown turning once. Drain on paper towels. Makes about 2 dozen hush puppies.

If you are on a float or camping trip, mix dry ingredients ahead in a plastic bag.

Floating on one of the beautiful streams of the Ozarks must be one of the most popular kinds of fun that Missourians enjoy. Some rugged types float anytime of the year, but most enjoy the months of April through October. A few safety tips:

1. Don't float alone.
2. Both floaters should know how to handle a canoe.
3. Life jackets should be worn by everyone.
4. If camping overnight, camp far enough away from the stream. There are often flash floods.
5. Pack clothes and supplies in waterproof bags. Spills are not uncommon.
6. Have fun and wear suntan lotion! Missouri sun can be hot.

SWEDISH PANCAKES
(Good for Sunday Brunch)

3 eggs, beaten
½ tsp. salt
1½ cup milk
¾ cup flour
3 Tbsp. sugar
3 Tbsp. melted butter

Beat eggs well and add sugar, salt, flour and milk. Add shortening and mix together. Batter will be thin.

Fry on griddle.

May be rolled with strawberry or other filling and sprinkled with powdered sugar.

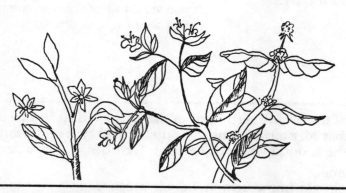

He was born in 1875 in the little town of Hamilton, Missouri. When his parents named him James "Cash" Penney, they didn't know how appropriate the name would be. His life epitomizes the American dream, which is that even if you are born poor you can become rich through hard work and perseverance. J. C. Penney Department Stores are famous throughout the country for giving good value for the dollar.

PECAN WAFFLES

2 cups sifted flour
4 tsp. baking powder
1 tsp. salt
2 cups milk
4 eggs, separated
1 cup melted butter or margarine
¾ cup coarsely chopped pecans

Heat waffle iron. Sift together flour, baking powder, salt and sugar, add pecans. Combine milk with slightly beaten egg yolks. Beat egg whites until stiff. Add egg yolk-milk mixture to dry ingredients. Beat just enough to moisten.

Stir in slightly cooled butter or margarine. Fold in egg whites until barely blended.

Pour batter from a pitcher onto hot waffle iron until batter is about 1" from edge. Close lid and do not open during baking.

Bake until steaming stops or indicator light goes on (about 4 minutes). Reheat waffle iron before making next waffles.

Makes about 8 waffles.

Wonderful served with maple butter!

It is a strange and wonderful sight to see thousands of bicyclists in the dead of night, quietly racing through the streets of St. Louis. They call it the Moonlight Ramble and Missourians of all ages join in the world's largest nightime bicycling event. When they finish, in the wee hours of the morning, they'll usually gather at friends' houses and sometimes make pecan waffles and then go home to sleep on a full stomach!

CORN FRITTERS
(Birds love em too!)

1½ cup all-purpose flour
2 tsp. baking powder
1 tsp. salt
½ tsp. pepper
½ cup milk
2 cups whole kernel corn
2 eggs, beaten
2 tbsp. butter, melted

Stir flour, baking powder, salt and pepper together in large bowl. Mix together milk, eggs, corn and butter and pour into dry ingredients.

Drop mixture by large spoonfuls into ½" of hot fat (375°).

Turn once and fry until golden.

Drain on paper towels and serve hot.

Makes 12 fritters.

John James Audubon, the great American naturalist, lived for a time in St. Genevieve, Missouri. He spent much of his time studying and sketching Missouri's many birds before returning to Kentucky. Several birds which he stuffed can be seen today in the local museum.

SWISS EGGS

½ lb. sliced Swiss cheese
1 cup whipping cream
6 eggs
salt, pepper, paprika to taste
refrigerator biscuits or toast
points

Heat oven to 425°.

Butter a deep 9" pie plate or similar baking dish. Line bottom and sides with overlapping slices of Swiss cheese to form a "crust".

Pour ½ cup cream into pan. Break eggs into pie, taking care that egg yolks remain whole.

Pour remaining cream over eggs. Salt and pepper to taste. Sprinkle with paprika.

Bake 15 to 20 minutes or until eggs are cooked to preference.

Serve immediately over split biscuits or toast points.

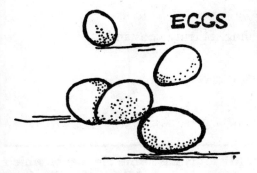

EGGS

The St. Louis Symphony Orchestra is the nation's second oldest orchestra. Playing in the beautiful Powell Hall, accompanied by chandeliers and velvet, the symphony presents a spectacular season of great music and internationally-known musical artists.

EASY ELEPHANT EGGS

1 dozen eggs
1 lb. bulk sausage
    corn flake crumbs

Hard boil eggs. Cool and shell. Mold sausage around eggs. Roll gently in corn flake crumbs.

Place in shallow baking pan or on a rack (a broiler pan is fine), and bake at 350° for 30 to 40 minutes.

Serve with choice of sauces.

Cheese Sauce:
1 cup sour cream
1 med. jar cheese whiz

Heat and stir. Do not boil.

Mushroom Sauce:
1 can cream of mushroom
    soup
1 cup half and half
3 drops tabasco sauce

Heat to boiling. Stirring constantly.

Circus elephants standing in a line is a fun sight. Missouri has some elephants which never move, but attract visitors from everywhere. Near Granite, Missouri is Elephant Rocks State Park. Huge boulders formed a billion years ago from molten rock look remarkably like a herd of elephants. Near the park is the oldest granite quarry in the state. Opened in 1869, it furnished stone for the Eads Bridge piers and cobbles for the streets of St. Louis.

MISSOURI HERITAGE QUILT DESIGN — **WHIGS DEFEAT**
MAKER: SALLIE ELLIOTT THOMAS 1846–1911

This section of Whigs Defeat, a Missouri quilt created by Sallie Elliot Thomas, glows in cool green and raspberry colors. Sallie's grandmother was the sister of Robert E. Lee.

Soups, Salads and Sandwiches

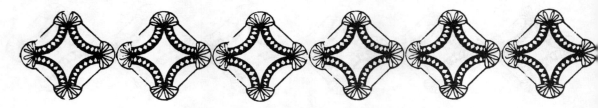

BARRELMAKERS STEAK SOUP
(Hearty and Filling)

2 tbsp. butter
1 cup sliced carrots
1 lb. ground chuck
2 cups tomato juice
1½ tsp. salt
4 cups milk
1 cup chopped onion
½ cup chopped celery
1 cup diced potatoes
1 tsp. seasoned salt
⅓ cup flour
⅛ tsp. pepper

Melt butter in a sauce pan, brown meat, add onion and cook until transparent. Stir in remaining ingredients except flour and milk. Cover and cook over low heat until vegetables are tender, about 20–25 min. Combine flour with 1 cup of the milk. Stir into soup mixture, boil a minute or so. Add remaining milk and heat, stirring frequently. Do not boil after adding milk.

Missouri has one of the only barrel making plants for wine in the country. The A & K Cooperage near Higbee, Mo. is known all over the United States for their fine oak barrels. They say that Missouri oak gives the best flavor to the wine.

GAZPACHO SOUP

2 cups tomato juice
6 peeled tomatoes (preferably home grown)
1 seeded chopped green pepper
1 peeled chopped onion
1 peeled chopped cucumber
2 tsp. chopped parsley
1 clove garlic, peeled
2 tbsp. olive oil
1 tbsp. salad oil
3 tbsp. red wine vinegar
1 tsp. salt

Place tomatoes, green pepper, onion and cucumber in a blender. Blend until smooth and pour into a large *glass* mixing bowl. Add remaining ingredients, mix and chill in refrigerator for several hours.

Soup may be garnished with a sprinkling of chopped raw green pepper, onion and cucumber.

The land which became the state of Missouri belonged, for a brief time, to the country of Spain. From 1770 to 1804, Spain held title to Missouri. Not very many material goods or buildings remain from that period, but we can try to imagine what our State was like in those days as we sip some Cold Gazpacho Soup.

LENTIL SOUP

1 cup lentils
8 cups water
1 potato, peeled & diced
3 carrots, pared & diced
1 onion, minced
½ cup sliced celery
1 lb. smoked sausage
1 tsp. salt
2 tbsp. flour
2 tbsp. butter

Soak lentils in water overnight. Cook over medium heat until tender adding more water if necessary. Add all ingredients except flour and butter. Cook about 20–30 minutes. Remove sausage and cool. Melt butter and add flour to make a roux. Add to soup to thicken. Remove skin from sausage, slice and add to soup. Heat and serve.

Very good with homemade bread.

The Amish are a simple people whose way of living takes us back to an earlier time. Horsedrawn buggies, wide brimmed hats and long dresses and bonnets represent a freedom of choice open to all Missourians. You can see the beauty and dignity of their lives if you visit Jamesport, Mo. Tours are available of the countryside. Amish women are known for their good home cooking, and a pot of lentil soup often bubbles happily away on a back burner.

CIOPPINO

1 lg. onion chopped (1 cup)
1 med. green pepper (chopped)
½ cup celery (sliced)
1 carrot, pared & shredded
3 cloves of garlic minced
3 tbsp. olive oil
2 cans (1 lb. each) tomatoes
1 can 8 oz. tomato sauce
1 tsp. leaf basil, crumbled
1 bay leaf
1 tsp. salt
¼ tsp. pepper
1 lb. fresh or frozen swordfish or halibut steak
1 doz. mussels or clams in shell
1½ cup dry white wine
1 8 oz. pkg. shrimp
½ lb. fresh or frozen scallops
2 tbsp. parsley, minced
1 lb. crab legs (optional)

Sauté onion, green pepper, celery, carrot & garlic in olive oil until soft. Stir in tomatoes, tomato sauce, basil, bay leaf, salt and pepper, heat to boiling. Reduce heat, cover and simmer for 2 hours. Discard bay leaf. While sauce simmers—clean fish & clams. Stir in wine and add fish. Simmer for 10 minutes. Add clams and cover. Steam 10 minutes or until done.

Ladle into soup bowl, sprinkle with parsley. Serve with sour dough bread or crusty French bread.

Missouri has long been the starting point for many great expeditions of discovery. Lewis and Clark's momentous trip during the years of 1804–1806, opened the vast reaches of the Northwest, and made Missouri the key to western exploration. Picture, if you will, Meriwether Lewis and William Clark sitting with their crew around a campfire in Oregon enjoying a fish stew, similar to this recipe for Cioppino.

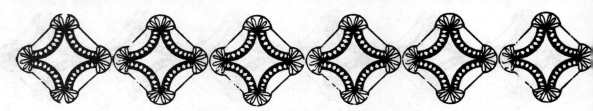

FUR TRAPPER CHEESE SOUP

1 small onion, chopped
2 tbsp. butter
¼ cup flour
2 cups chicken broth
2 cups milk or half and half
½ cup finely diced carrots
¼ cup finely diced celery
¼ tsp. salt
   dash paprika
1 cup diced sharp process
   cheese

Cook onion, carrots and celery in butter until tender but not brown. Blend in flour. Slowly add broth and then milk or cream, salt and paprika and cheese.

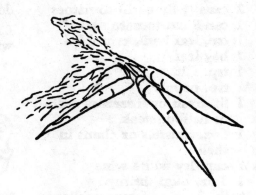

Fur trading was very important in Missouri's early history. Traders in the early days took their fine furs—mink, otter, beavers and martens to Montreal or Quebec and deerskins and buffalo hides were taken to New Orleans.

While the traders were up in Canada they would sit around and swap tales of the wilderness and usually enjoy a big bowl of cheese soup.

CREAM OF PUMPKIN SOUP
(or what to do with the Halloween pumpkin)

2 lbs. pumpkin—peeled,
    seeded and cubed
salt and pepper
2 ribs of celery, diced
4 cups milk
2 cups chicken stock
1 tsp. lemon juice
2 tbsp. butter

Season the pumpkin with salt and pepper. Put into a large sauce pan with celery. Cover with milk and stock and simmer until pumpkin is soft—about 30-40 minutes.

Remove from heat and pour in batches into blender. Blend until smooth. Return to pan and add butter. Taste for seasoning.

You may add honey (about 1 tbsp.) and sprinkle with nutmeg if desired. Cooked pumpkin sours quite easily and soup should be used the day it is made or the day after.

The land of the Ozark Mountains in southern Missouri is from 1.2 billion to 1.4 billion years old. Parts of the Ozarks have been said to be from the Precambrian period—the oldest lands in the Continent.

They are not as rugged as the Rocky Mountains but their beauty, mineral deposits and isolation lured many an early settler to the area. The earliest settlers took cooking lessons from the Indians in the area and made Pumpkin Soup on chilly fall days.

SUMMERTIME POTATO SALAD
(Good Anytime)

1 cup mayonnaise
2 tbsp. vinegar
1½ tsp. salt
1 tsp. sugar
¼ tsp. pepper
1 tbsp. prepared mustard
4 cups cooked, peeled and cubed potatoes (about 6 medium)
1 cup sliced celery
½ cup chopped onion
3 hard cooked eggs, shelled and chopped

In large bowl, mix together first 6 ingredients until smooth. Add remaining ingredients tossing well. Cover and chill at least 4 hours. Makes about 5 cups.

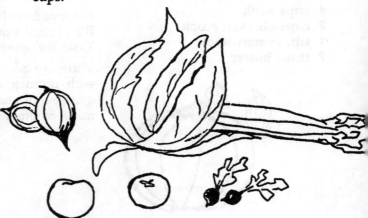

At the turn of the century, the outstanding recreational area in Missouri was South of Warrensberg. It was called Pertle Springs. The mineral springs were rich in iron and sulphur and supposedly had healing powers. Hundreds of people visited the site, including Billy Sunday, Carrie Nations, Buffalo Bill and William Jennings Bryan.

GERMAN POTATO SALAD

This was made along with wine in many a home in Hermann!

3 lbs. red potatoes, about 6 large, boiled, peeled and sliced
12 slices bacon
2 tbsp. flour
2 tsp. salt
½ tsp. celery seed
¾ cup water
1 medium onion, peeled and diced
4 tbsp. sugar
½ tsp. pepper
⅓ cup wine vinegar

Dice bacon and fry until crisp. Remove bacon and cook onion in bacon grease until transparent.

Stir in flour, sugar, salt and pepper and celery seed.

Cook over low heat, add water and vinegar, boil for 1 minute.

Add bacon and potatoes stirring gently to coat potatoes.

Serve warm, with Missouri country ham.

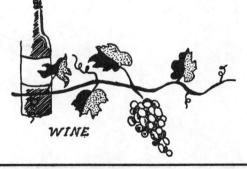

WINE

Before prohibition ended wine production in Missouri, the state was making and shipping more than 3 million gallons of wine a year. Stone Hill Winery in Hermann, Missouri was the third largest winery in the world and the second largest in the United States.

LUCKY LINDY'S SALMON SALAD

1 cup carrots, grated
2 tbsp. onions, minced
½ cup celery, diced
½ cup salad dressing, or
  mayonnaise
2 tbsp. cream
2 tbsp. prepared mustard
1 large can salmon, drained
  and cleaned
1 can shoe string potatoes

Mix first seven ingredients together. Top with shoe string potatoes before serving.

Charles Lindbergh took off from Lambert St. Louis Airfield in St. Louis on May 12, 1927. It was the first step in the trans-Atlantic flight from New York to Paris. His plane was called the "Spirit of St. Louis" and his financial backing came from St. Louis businessmen.

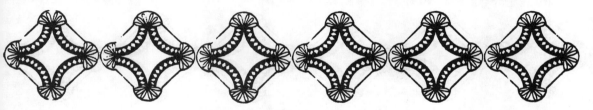

COLD PEA SALAD

1 package (1 lb.) frozen peas, cooked and drained
5 hard boiled eggs, chopped fine
1 onion, diced
1 small green pepper, seeded and diced fine
6 stalks celery, sliced very fine
8 oz. cheddar cheese, diced fine
   salt, pepper to taste
1 cup mayonnaise

Mix ingredients gently together, blend well and refrigerate.

Iced tea is *the* summertime drink in Missouri. They say it began during the World's Fair Exposition of 1904. It seems that vendors were selling hot tea at a stand. There was a new-fangled ice making machine which gathered crowds right next door. It was summertime, hot and humid, and someone got the bright idea of putting a chunk of ice in his hot tea!

ORIENTAL BROCCOLI SALAD

2 bunches fresh broccoli
2½ qts water
2 tbsp. oil
1 tbsp. salt
1 can water chestnuts, drained and sliced

Sauce:

2 tbsp. light soy sauce
1 tbsp. sugar
2 tbsp. white wine vinegar
2 tbsp. sesame oil (or regular)
¼ tsp. salt

Cut the broccoli into 2 parts, the flower part and the stem part. Cut the flower part into small bite size clusters. Peel the tough skin off the stem and quarter the stem lengthwise. Slantcut each quarter into 2 inch pieces.

In a large pot bring to a rapid boil the water, oil and salt. Add the broccoli and boil quickly for 1 minute. Drain, and rinse in cold water and drain again. Place on large platter.

Make sauce, adding water chestnuts. Pour over broccoli and toss together. Chill several hours.

The Missouri Botanical Garden founded by Henry Shaw in 1859 in St. Louis was the first of its kind in the U. S. Known around the world today for its research programs and excellence in horticulture, it has a 14 acre Japanese Garden which is considered the finest outside Japan.

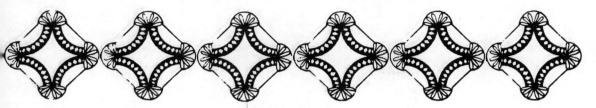

WILTED LETTUCE SALAD

1 bunch leaf lettuce (or substitute greens of your choice)
4 slices bacon, diced
½ cup water
½ cup cider vinegar
1 egg, well-beaten
3 tbsp. sugar
½ tsp. salt
3 scallions, finely sliced

Wash lettuce and drain. Tear into bite sized pieces.

Fry bacon until crisp in large skillet. Leaving bacon in skillet, remove all but ¼ cup of bacon fat. Add other ingredients to bacon and fat.

Bring to boil. Pour hot dressing over lettuce and turn several times.

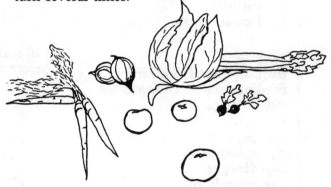

The Battle of Wilson's Creek, fought in 1861, 10 miles southwest of Springfield, Missouri, was one of the most important fought in Missouri during the Civil War. While losses were about equal on both sides, the Confederates were technically the winners. A marker placed on the site honors the "hundreds of brave men, North and South, who on this field, died for the right as God gave them to see the right".

SPINACH SALAD

Mix Together:

1½ lbs. fresh spinach trimmed
    and washed
½ pkg. dry Pepperidge herb
    dressing (stuffing mix)
1 lb. bacon fried crisp
    (crumbled)
6 hard boiled eggs (sliced)

Dressing:

3 tbsp. prepared mustard
1 medium onion chopped fine
⅔ cup of sugar
1 tsp. salt
½ tsp. pepper
1 tsp. celery seed
½ cup vinegar
½ cup mazola oil

Mix all ingredients in mixer. Pour over spinach ½ hr. before serving.

FRESH VEGETABLE SALAD

1 head of cauliflower
1 head of broccoli
10 whole mushrooms
½ red onion, diced
8 slices cooked bacon, diced,
  save bacon grease
¼ cup red wine vinegar
½ cup sugar
¾ cup mayonnaise
1½ cup sour cream
  salt and pepper

Slice and clean fresh vegetables (flowerets only). Add bacon drippings and chopped bacon to sour cream and mayonnaise mixture. Add red wine and sugar to the above. Refrigerate 2 to 3 hours.

This salad should be served the same day as mixed.

Ulysses S. Grant, who was the 18th President of the United States, lived on a farm south of St. Louis. His cabin is the only surviving residence handbuilt by an American President. The farm today is open to the public. It is owned by August A. Busch Jr., and is a favorite place to visit for Missourians of all ages. There are animals and bird shows, a small animal feeding and petting area and a wild game preserve.

MARINATED VEGETABLE SALAD

1 16 oz. can French style
  green beans, drained
1 8 oz. can baby peas, drained
1 cup celery, cut up fine
1 green pepper, seeded and
  sliced
1 medium onion, peeled and
  sliced very fine
1 sm. jar pimento, drained
  and chopped

Dressing:

  1 cup cider vinegar
  1 cup sugar
  ½ cup salad oil
  ½ tsp. salt

Combine vinegar, sugar, oil and salt and stir until sugar is dissolved. Mix all vegetables together. Pour dresing over vegetables and toss well. Refrigerate overnight and drain when ready to serve.

Missouri is made up of four different types of land. In the northern part of the state are the "glaciated plains", rich flat land formed by ancient glaciers. To the west are the "great plains", land which was not created by glaciers. In the very southern most part of the state is the area known as delta land, the land formed by the great Mississippi River. The fourth unique land area is the Ozark Mountain Region.

COLD PASTA SALAD

1 pkg. spinach noodles,
    cooked and drained
1 pkg. fettucine noodles
2 jars artichoke hearts, cut
    into quarters, with juice
1 can pitted black olives,
    drained and quartered
2 stalks broccoli, flowerets only
10– 12 green onions, cut into ½"
    pieces
3 cloves garlic, pressed &
    minced
¼ cup olive oil (or a combina-
    tion of salad and olive oil
    for a milder taste)
¼ cup lemon juice
2 tbsp. worcestershire sauce
1 tbsp. fine herbs
2 tsp. tabasco sauce
1 tsp. oregano
½ lb. hard salami, cut into
    julienne strips

Put everything but the pasta in a bowl and cover. Refrigerate 1–2 hours. Add cooked and drained noodles. Refrigerate overnight, garnish with halved cherry tomatoes. Serve cold. Serves 6

Missouri has its own "yellow brick road", a 50 mile stretch of highway from Vandalia to Fulton. Along Highway 54 lie 8 major plants which produce firebrick—those very special bricks which can resist very high temperatures. They are used for many purposes, including paving and launching pads for our nation's space program.

This cool pasta salad will lower your temperature.

FIVE CUP FRUIT SALAD
(AMBROSIA)

Mix Together:

- 1 cup Mandarin oranges
- 1 cup pineapple tidbits
- 1 cup coconut
- 1 cup miniature marsh-
  mallows
- 1 cup sour cream

Mix and refrigerate for at least 2 hours or overnight.

William Woods College in Fulton, Mo., is a fine school for women. It is somewhat unusual because a whole field of study is devoted to horsemanship. The school maintains a stable of over 75 thoroughbred horses and its own show arena and riding courses. Because of this, and its other attributes, the school attracts young women from all over the United States and abroad.

This is a recipe that's a favorite with young ladies—young men too!

LIME SALAD

1 package lime jello
½ cup boiling water
1 small package cream cheese
1½ cup cold milk
1 small can crushed pineapple, drained

Dissolve jello in boiling water. Cool to room temperature.

Pour into blender, add cream cheese and milk, blend until smooth.

Pour into mold and add pineapple. Chill until set.

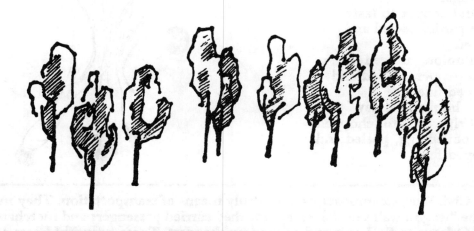

Just west of St. Genevieve, Missouri are huge deposits of lime. Mississippi Lime Company is one of the worlds largest producers of lime.

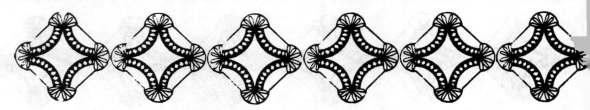

MARGE'S VINAIGRETTE DRESSING

2 cups oil
¾ cup vinegar (red wine or cider)
½ cup water
2 to 3 tbsp. worcestershire sauce
3 tbsp. ketchup
⅔ cup sugar
salt and pepper to taste
1 clove garlic, peeled and minced
1 small onion, minced
1 green pepper, seeded and chopped fine
2 tbsp. chopped parsley
1 small ripe tomato, chopped
1 hard boiled egg, peeled and chopped fine

Shake or mix all ingredients well. Refrigerate.

Before the Civil War, steamboats were the only means of transportation. They might be called the "wagon trains of the water" for they carried passengers and merchandise from New Orleans to St. Louis and opened up the west. These beautiful boats could be heard before they were seen with their bells and whistles announcing to the world that they were on the way.

CELERY SEED DRESSING

⅔ cup sugar
¼ tsp. salt
1 tsp. dry mustard
1 small onion, grated
1 cup salad oil
5 tbsp. vinegar
1 tbsp. lemon juice
½ cup honey
1 tsp. celery seed
1 tsp. paprika

Place all ingredients in blender and blend until well mixed.

Serve over fresh fruit salad.

Salt was a valuable and necessary commodity to the early settlers. Daniel Boone's sons manufactured salt by boiling saline spring water, packing the salt in canoes, and floating it to St. Louis. The spring is known today as Boone's Lick.

MISSOURI MAYFAIR DRESSING

2 large ribs celery, cut in 2" pieces.
¼ cup prepared mustard
1 can anchovies, strips
1 tsp. pepper
1 large clove garlic
3 eggs, added one at a time
2 cups oil

Put first 5 ingredients in blender on high speed until mixed.

Add one egg at a time until well blended.

Add oil one cup at a time until well blended and mixture becomes thick.

Pour over salad.

Members of the Church of the Latter Day Saints, more commonly known as Mormons settled for a time near Independence, Missouri. Joseph Smith, the prophet of the church, had a vision showing that Missouri was to be the "new Zion". Persecution of the Mormons led them to seek a new location.

FRENCH SALAD DRESSING

1 cup salad oil
½ cup cider vinegar
⅓ cup catsup
½ cup sugar
  juice of one lemon
1 tsp. salt
1 tsp paprika
1 small onion grated

Place all ingredients in a blender and beat until well blended. Refrigerate.

The oldest town in Missouri is Ste. Genevieve, founded in 1735, by the French. Bolduc House, located there, is an example of the architecture and construction of the period. The vertical log walls covered with plaster, solid stone chimneys and an overhanging roof which forms a wide porch, a style common to the period. The porches lent a graciousness to the rough life of the early settlers and a place where the beauties of the land could be seen.

AUTO BUILDER'S FAVORITE SANDWICH

Dark Rye Bread
Thousand Island Dressing
sliced cooked chicken breast
crisp fried bacon
peeled sliced avocado
lettuce leaves
tomato slices

For each serving, place 2 slices of bread on a cutting board. Spread each with Thousand Island dressing. Top 1 slice of bread with lettuce leaf, 2 tomato slices, 2 bacon slices, 4 avocado slices, add 3 to 4 slices of cooked chicken and top with bread.

Serve extra Thousand Island dressing on side.

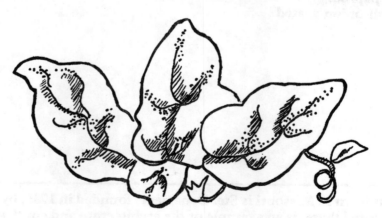

Kansas City, Missouri is second only to Detroit in the production of automobiles in the United States.

SHRIMPBURGERS

1 **can of shrimp**
½ **cup finely chopped celery**
¼ **cup finely chopped green**
   pepper
1 **tbsp. grated onion**
1 **cup grated cheese**
⅓ **cup mayonnaise**

Put ingredients through food chopper.

Spread on half of a hamburger bun. Put strip of fried bacon on top.

Bake until cheese is melted in a 350° oven.

Makes 15.

They come from far and near to see whose tractor is the strongest. It is the Western National Tractor Pull, held each July in Bethany. The owners of the tractors have worked for months fine tuning their machines hoping to win first prize.

MISSOURI HERITAGE QUILT DESIGN — **ROSE BUD**
MAKER: SUSAN STROTHERS SHAW 1856–1926

Many girls in Missouri families were taught to quilt at a very young age. Women dyed their own fabrics and many Missouri families used this design, from generation to generation.

Entrees

FRIED FISH

catfish filets (or crappie, bass or trout)
cornmeal
all purpose flour
salt/pepper
½ cup salad oil
¼ cup butter
½ cup cold milk
1 egg, beaten

Rinse and dry fish.

Mix 1 cup cornmeal with ½ cup flour, 1 tsp. salt and ½ tsp. pepper. Beat egg into milk. Dip fish filets into egg/milk wash and then into cornmeal/flour mixture.

Heat oil and butter in frying pan until sizzling (350°) and about ¼″ deep.

Place fish in fat and fry about 6 to 8 minutes on each side. Lower heat and fry about 5 minutes or until fish flakes easily with a fork. Drain and serve immediately with Tartar Sauce.

★Note! Catfish can be marinated in Buttermilk to give a fresh taste to the fish.

If you just happen to be down in Nixa, Mo. on a Friday in May and all the town businesses, offices and schools are closed, don't think that you've forgotten an official holiday. These good folks are celebrating Sucker Day. Everyone closes up shop and goes fishing for suckers. These fresh water, bony, white fleshed fish are considered delicacies in Southern Missouri.

If you don't have any suckers, but you have caught some catfish or some bass or crappies you might want to fix them this way.

TARTAR SAUCE

1 tbsp. chopped capers (optional)
1 tbsp. chopped green olives
1 tbsp. chopped parsley
2 tbsp. sweet pickle relish (or
  chopped sweet pickles)
1 tbsp. minced onion or
  shallots
1 hard boiled egg, finely
  chopped
1 cup mayonnaise

Mix all ingredients and chill thoroughly. You may
thin with a little lemon juice.

BEER BARBEQUE SAUCE

2 cups tomato paste
1½ cups water or beer
½ cup minced onion
½ cup dill relish
1 tsp. Liquid Smoke
1 tsp. black pepper
2 tsp. bar-b-que spice

Saute onions, add tomato paste and stir in water or beer. Blend in all other ingredients and simmer. Thicken with cornstarch to desired consistency.

Beer barbeque sauce is traditional with pork steaks. Marinate pork steaks in a mixture of 1 cup vinegar and 1 cup water for several hours. Remove from marinade and grill over hot coals. When cooked to well done baste with Beer Barbeque Sauce.

NOTE: If a sweeter sauce is desired, add:

¼ cup brown sugar and
3 tablespoons vinegar to Barbeque Sauce.

Anheuser Busch Brewery, located in St. Louis, is the world's largest brewery. Constructed in 1870, the Brew House, the Clydesdale Stables and main office building have been designated National Historic Landmarks.

BEEF ROULADES (BEEF ROLLS)

2½ lb. round steak (pounded thin)
1 cup chopped onions
sliced bacon
1 cup bread crumbs
ground paprika
ground mace
ground cloves
ground rosemary
ground salt
ground pepper
dill pickles
bay leaf
1 cup beef broth
½ cup red wine (optional)

Cut beef into strips 3" wide by 6" long. Sprinkle each strip with spices, place 1 piece of bacon on meat and then about 1 tbsp. bread crumbs and 1 tbsp. chopped onion. Roll up and secure with string or toothpick.

If desired, about half the beef rolls may be seasoned with spices and then, instead of bacon & onion; substitute a dill pickle.

In large heavy frying pan, brown beef rolls in about 3 tbsp. oil until brown on all sides. Place beef rolls in ovenproof casserole, add 1 can beef broth, 1 bay leaf and if desired ½ cup red wine.

Bake in moderate oven 350° for about 1 hour.

Remove toothpicks or string before serving and thicken gravy with 4 tbsp. flour mixed with a little cold water and a dark rye bread crust.

Serve with buttered noodles.

The whole town is a National Historic Site. Nestled in the rolling hills and forests by the Missouri River, the area reminded the first German settlers of their homeland. Hermann, Missouri was named for a first Century A.D. German general. The early colonists tried to preserve their heritage by teaching German in the schools. Today, residents are still proud of their heritage and share it through Maifests and Oktoberfests, with their fellow Missourians.

SPACE TRIP CABBAGE ROLLS

1 **large head cabbage**	Core cabbage and cook in large pot of boiling water until just tender. Remove from water and cool until able to handle.
1½ **lb. ground chuck**	
¾ **cup long-grained white rice, uncooked**	
1 **tsp. cinnamon**	Mix together hamburger, rice, cinnamon, mustard, salt and pepper, egg, worcestershire sauce and onion.
1 **tbsp. mustard, prepared**	
1 **large can tomatoes**	
salt and pepper to taste	Place spoonful of meat mixture on a cabbage leaf, roll up and place in ovenproof casserole.
1 **egg**	
1 **tsp. worcestershire sauce**	Cover with tomatoes and ½ can water.
1 **small onion, diced very fine**	Bake at 350° for 1½ hours.

Missourians are justifiably proud of having manufactured the space capsule which carried astronaut John Glenn safely through the nation's first manned orbital flight in 1962. The McDonnell-Douglas Corporation manufactured that capsule and many other spacecrafts at their plant in St. Louis.

VEAL SCALOPPINE

2 lbs. veal, thinly sliced and
  pounded
⅓ cup flour
  salt and pepper
¼ cup corn oil or peanut oil
1 cup sliced fresh mushrooms
1 med. green pepper, seeded
  and sliced
4 shallots, peeled and sliced
  (or substitute regular onions)
½ cup dry sherry or Marsala
  wine
2 tbsp. water
2 tbsp. tomato sauce

Season the veal medallions with salt and pepper. Dredge in flour. Heat oil in large frying pan. Brown veal quickly on both sides. Add mushrooms, green peppers and shallots or onions. Cook until vegetables are soft and transparent. Drain off excess oil. Add sherry or wine. Simmer for 5 minutes. Add water and tomato sauce. Simmer 5 minutes more. Serves 4.

Missouri just might be able to say that it saved the world's grapevines. More than a century ago when vineyards all over the world were decimated with phylloxera, Missouri's hardy root stock was grafted onto the ailing vines and saved them from extinction. Herman Jaeger, a Missourian who sent France 17 carloads of rootings, was given the Cross of the French Legion of Honor.

SCALLOPED OYSTERS

1½ pts. oysters
3 cups cracker crumbs, rolled
¾ cups melted butter
1⅛ cup light cream
⅜ cup oyster liquid
⅜ tsp. worcestershire sauce
¾ tsp. salt

Drain oysters reserving ⅜ cup liquid. Combine cracker crumbs and butter and spread ⅓ of crumbs on bottom of an 8″ × 8″ pan.

Cover with half the oysters. Sprinkle with pepper. Spread another layer (1 cup) of crumbs and cover with remaining oysters, sprinkle with pepper.

Combine cream, oyster liquid, worcestershire sauce and salt. Pour mixture over oysters and top with remaining crumbs.

Bake at 350° for 40 minutes.

Kansas City is host to a most unusual industry. The "Great Midwest Corporation" leases huge underground caves to over 100 different businesses. Companies use the caves for food storage as well as industrial storage. These limestone caverns are 270 million years old and could shelter 1.3 million people in case of a nuclear attack.

TAUM SAUK TOLERINI

1 lb. noodles
2 large onions
2 large green peppers
2 cloves garlic
2 lbs. ground chuck
2 medium cans tomatoes
1 can whole kernel corn, or
1 cup fresh
2 tbsp. chili powder
1 lb. American cheddar cheese
1 can ripe olives, with liquid

Cook noodles. Brown beef. Saute finely cut onion, peppers and garlic. Salt and pepper to taste.

Combine all except ½ of cheese. Mix together and put into casserole.

Top with remaining cheese.

Bake in slow oven, 350° for 1½ hours.

If you're feeling fit, you might want to try the 20 mile backpacking trail over Taum Sauk Mountain. Taum Sauk is Missouri's highest point at 1,772 feet.

MISSOURI QUAIL BIRDS

6 quails, cleaned
¾ cup butter
3 ribs celery
1 onion
6 slices bacon
  brandy
  juice of 1 orange
  juice of 1 lemon
  chopped parsley
2 tbsp. honey

Sauce:

½ cup melted butter
  juice of 1 lemon
  juice of 1 orange
2 tbsp. chopped parsley
2 tbsp. honey

Butter a 9" casserole. Place a small piece of butter inside each quail along with a small piece of celery and a small piece of onion. Wrap quail in bacon and secure with toothpicks and place breast side down in baking dish. Place rest of onion and celery around quails. Sprinkle birds with brandy.

Bake at 350° for 1 hour. Baste quails every 15 minutes with the sauce.

Heat all together and brush over quails with a pastry brush.

After baking, remove quail and keep warm. Remove toothpicks. Take 2 tbsp. flour and add to pan drippings, cook slowly and add ½ cup water, 1 cup heavy cream and 2 tbsp. current jelly. Do not boil! Take from heat and add 3 tbsp. brandy to sauce.

Pour small amount around quails and the rest in a sauceboat.

Missouri is a hunter's paradise. Ever since the days of Daniel Boone, the variety and abundance of game has attracted sportsmen. Quail can be found most everywhere, along with the wild turkey. Whitetail deer, squirrels and cottontail rabbits are also favorite targets, but Missouri leads the nation in raccoon hunting.

STEAMBOAT SOLE

¾ cup butter
1 clove garlic, peeled and minced
1 small onion, chopped
¼ cup green pepper, chopped fine
12 large shrimp, cooked and cleaned
¼ cup bread crumbs
1 tbsp. chopped parsley
½ tsp. salt
  dash pepper
1½ lbs. sole
3 egg yolks
2 tbsp. fresh lemon juice
  dash cayenne

In large skillet melt 2 tbsp. butter. Stir in garlic, onion and green pepper. Saute until tender.

Dice 8 shrimp, add to vegetables along with parsley, bread crumbs, salt and pepper and remove from heat.

Spread about 2 tbsp. of shrimp mixture on sole filets and roll.

Place fish in baking dish into which 2 tbsp. butter has been melted.

Bake at 350° for 25 to 30 minutes.

Top with blender Hollandaise.

Melt ½ cup butter. In blender container place egg yolks and lemon juice, ¼ tsp. salt and cayenne pepper. Blend on low and immediately pour melted butter in thin stream and blend on low until all butter is added.

Place baked fish on a platter and pour Hollandaise over. Garnish with remaining shrimp.

The Great Mississippi Steamboat Race of 1870 was really something to see. In the end, the Robert E. Lee was the winner, but only because the Natchez had become lost in the fog near Cairo, Illinois. All along the river, from New Orleans to St. Louis, for three historic days, people came to watch the great boats battling it out.

PLAYERS' FAVORITE PEPPER ROAST

3 lbs. arm chuck roast or
    sirloin
1 tsp. salt
¼ cup peppercorns—cracked
    with rolling pin
1 cup wine vinegar
½ cup salad oil
3 tbsp. lemon juice
1 sm. onion, chopped
2 tsp. oregano
1 tsp. rosemary
1 bay leaf

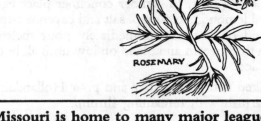

ROSEMARY

Mix all marinade ingredients together. Place meat in shallow glass baking dish. Pour marinade over, cover and refrigerate for 2 hours. Turn meat often. Remove meat and place on cutting board and pound half of crushed peppercorns into each side of roast or steak.

Grill over hot coals until juice appears. Turn and grill until desired doneness.

Return to cutting board and carve diagonally. Serves 4.

Missouri is home to many major league sports teams. Football has the Kansas City Chiefs and the St. Louis Cardinals. Soccer, the Comets from Kansas City and the Streamers from St. Louis. Hockey boasts the St. Louis Blues. But baseball is really a favorite sport in Missouri and the states two great teams battled it out in the World Series in 1985. The St. Louis Cardinals and the Kansas City Royals played long and hard—while the Royals won, the Cardinals say that they'll wait for another day!

CHICKEN ASPARAGUS CASSEROLE

12 **sliced cooked chicken, preferably breast meat**
1 lb. cooked asparagus
3 cups canned condensed cream of mushroom soup
1 cup cream (half & half)
1 tsp. curry powder
4 drops tabasco sauce
4 tbsp. chopped pimento
4 tbsp. grated Parmesan cheese
paprika

Place asparagus in buttered shallow baking dish. Arrange chicken slices over asparagus. Combine soup, cream, curry powder and 4 drops tabasco. Heat, stirring constantly until smooth. Add pimento. Pour over chicken and asparagus, sprinkle with cheese and paprika. Bake in a hot oven at 400° for 15 minutes. Serves 6.

The first circuit court in Boone County was an open-air court, not an unusual occurrance for the times. What was somewhat unusual was the first case heard in the court. It seems that there was a bounty of $1.50 at the time for wolf scalps. A scheming hunter thought he would take the one scalp he caught and make it two with a sharp knife, thereby doubling his money. He was caught, tried and fined $5.00. The tree under which the case was tried, still stands today near Columbia, Missouri.

SHOW ME STATES BARBEQUE SHRIMP

2 lbs. raw shrimp, peeled & deveined
1 cup vegetable oil
1 tbsp. brown sugar
1 tsp. salt
1 tsp. dry mustard
1 tbsp. worcestershire sauce
¼ tsp. liquid smoke
½ cup red dry wine
 juice of one lemon

Combine all ingredients but shrimp in a baking dish and add shrimp. Marinate for ½ hour or more. Remove from marinade and broil over hot coals.

*Broiling tip: Place some dried grapevines over coals to give more flavor to shrimp.

A long forgotten Congressman from Missouri first coined the immortal words that everyone associates with the State. He stood up in Congress in 1889 and addressed the members. "Gentlemen, frothy eloquence neither convinces nor satisfies me. I am from Missouri, you have got to show me". His name was William Vandiver and his sentiments are echoed today from border to border.

STUDENTS' CHOP SUEY

1 lb. round steak, cut in very
  thin strips (easier to cut
  when semi-frozen)
2 tbsp. salad oil
1½ cups sliced fresh mushrooms
1½ cups diagonally sliced celery
1 cup green pepper, seeded
  and cut into squares
½ cup green onion, cut into 1"
  pieces
½ cup bean sprouts
1 can beef broth
2 tbsp. soy sauce
2 tbsp. cornstarch
½ cup water
  cooked rice

In large skillet brown beef in oil. Add vegetables, broth and soy sauce. Cover and cook until vegetables are tender crisp, about 20 minutes. Stir occasionally. Blend cornstarch and water, stir into sauce. Cook stirring until thickened. Serve over rice. Makes 4 servings.

The people of the Ozarks pride themselves on their independence and self-reliance. Young people follow in these traditions. At the School of the Ozarks, all students are required to work for their own room and board by doing various campus jobs. A college education comes to have real meaning for these hard-working students.

TROUT AMANDINE

4 trout, cleaned and scaled
½ cup butter
   flour
2 eggs, beaten
¼ cup slivered blanched
   almonds
¼ cup white wine
   juice of one lemon
   salt and pepper

Wash trout in cold water, wipe with paper towels.

In large skillet, melt butter and heat until very hot but not burning.

Dip trout in egg wash and then flour. Saute over medium heat until golden brown, about 5 minutes on each side.

Remove from skillet and place on serving dish. Keep warm in 250° oven.

Add almonds to skillet and brown. Add wine and lemon juice and salt and pepper.

Cook until slightly thickened scraping bits from pan. Pour over trout and serve.

Serves 4.

Trout fishermen compete with each other for the coveted "Slippery Liz" prize. No—Slippery Liz is not a lady. She's a red rubber worm, the prize of the Rose Holland Trout Derby held every October in Montauk State Park.

RABBIT STEW
(a favorite with early settlers)

1 rabbit, 3 to 4 pounds, can be purchased at your local store
¼ lb. bacon, diced
1 tbsp. butter
½ lb. mushrooms, cleaned and sliced
2 onions, peeled and diced
1 cup beef broth
1 cup red wine
1 tbsp. minced parsley
4 carrots, sliced
1 bay leaf
   salt and pepper
2 tbsp. flour

Marinate rabbit in the wild game marinade—see recipe on page 177—for 24 hours.

Remove from marinade and drain.

In large heavy skillet or Dutch oven cook bacon in butter until bacon crisps, then saute rabbit pieces browning on all sides.

Add mushrooms and onion and cook until onion browns. Add flour to make a roux. Remove from heat, add beef broth, wine, parsley, carrots and bay leaf.

Return to heat and simmer 2 hours.

Serves 6

The land of the Ozarks was included in the Louisiana Purchase and sold in those olden days for 12 cents an acre.

LAUGHING SPAGHETTI SAUCE

1 cup chopped onion
3 cloves garlic—minced
1 tsp. salt
½ tsp. pepper
2 tbsp. sugar
½ cup pure olive oil (extra virgin)
1 tsp. sweet basil
½ tsp. oregano
2 tbsp. chopped parsley
2 6 oz. cans tomato paste
1 lg. can Italian tomatoes
½ cup burgundy wine
½ cup water

Saute onion and garlic in hot oil for about 5 minutes or until transparent. Add remaining ingredients and simmer for 1 to 1½ hours.

(If desired, brown 1 lb. of Italian sausage, drain and add to sauce).

Serve over cooked spaghetti noodles and serve with freshly grated parmesan cheese.

What child, now long grown, doesn't remember a sad faced clown who won his way into every American's heart? Emmett Kelly, playing his world-famous "Weary Willie", came from the little Missouri town of Houston.

K. C. STOCKYARD MEAT BALLS

½ cup finely chopped onion
2 tbsp. butter
½ cup seasoned bread crumbs
⅓ cup water
1 lb. ground chuck
1 tbsp. chopped parsley
3 tbsp. grated Parmesan cheese
1 egg, slightly beaten
1 tsp. salt
¼ tsp. pepper
1 tbsp. worcestershire sauce
¼ tsp. garlic powder

Saute onion in butter until tender.

Mix all together and roll into small balls about the size of ping pong balls.

Place on a lipped cookie sheet and bake at 375° for 20-25 minutes.

The Kansas City Stockyards were first opened in 1871 and were at the start simply used as a rest area for cattle on their trek from Abilene to Chicago. Today the number of animals averages 255 million a year, which makes Kansas City a major feed and stock market.

BELGIAN BEEF CASSEROLE

3½– 4 lbs top round steak or
    rump roast, cut into 2″
    cubes
  3 lb. onions, cubed
  ¼ cup sugar
  2 bottles beer
  2 cups beef broth

Bouquet Garni:
  1 rib celery
  1 leek
  1 carrot
  1 bay leaf
  ½ tsp. thyme
  ¼ cup butter, 3 tbsp. oil
    salt & pepper

Season beef and brown in hot heavy skillet in butter and oil until very brown. Remove beef and saute onions until very brown. Add sugar and deglaze with beer. Add bouquet garni and beef broth and cook for 2 hours. Make 1 slice of toast—spread with Dijon mustard and add to mixture.

Serve with boiled potatoes or buttered noodles.

BAY

The U. S. Navy has brought her out of mothballs. She is the U. S. S. Missouri or "Mighty Mo" as she is affectionately known. Old Mo has seen some momentous moments. Gen. Douglas MacArthur accepted the unconditional surrender of the Japanese at the end of the Second World War on her deck. MacArthur said to Americans, "Let us pray that peace be now restored to the world and that God will preserve it always". Noble words which would be appropriate for today as well.

FRIED HAM AND RED-EYED GRAVY

Slice ham about ¼ to ½ in. thick. Cut gashes in fat to keep ham from curling. Place slices in a heavy skillet and cook until ham is brown. Remove from pan and keep warm. To the drippings in the skillet, add about ½ cup hot water; cook until gravy turns red. A little strong coffee might be added to deepen the color.

If you wish to bake a whole country ham, scrub outside of ham well, and soak overnight. Bake to your preference.

If you visit the Ozarks today, you might be lucky enough to hear some genuine fiddle music. Shaped note hymnals can still be found in the Ozarks. Shaped notes are used to facilitate sightreading and singing without accompaniment.

BALLOON RACE MOSTACIOLLI

½ lb. pork sausage
1 lb. ground beef
3 medium onion, chopped
6 ribs of celery, chopped
3 green peppers, chopped
½ lb. moderately sharp cheese
1 can tomato soup
1 lb. small shell noodles
1 small jar pimento
½ lb. mushrooms, sliced
3 tsp. salt or more to taste
1½ tsp. pepper
2 tbsp. chili powder
3 tbsp. butter

Brown meat, remove from pan, drain off fat. Add butter and saute vegetables until translucent.

Melt cheese in soup. Boil noodles in salted water until just tender, about 12-15 minutes. Drain.

Combine all ingredients in large ovenproof casserole or roaster and bake for 30 to 40 minutes at 325°.

If mixture seems dry, add small can of tomato sauce.

Serves 4-6.

The sky is full of beautiful colorful balloons—big hot air balloons. It is the annual Great Forest Park Balloon Race. The tradition of balloon races in St. Louis started back during the time of the World's Fair, when the balloons were gas powered.

HOME FRONT BEEF STEW

1½- 2 lbs. boneless chuck steak
⅓ cup flour
1 tsp. salt
  pepper
1 tsp. dry mustard
1 tsp. paprika
1 bay leaf
¼ cup salad oil
6 potatoes, peeled and cut into large cubes
8 carrots, peeled and cut into large cubes
6 celery ribs, peeled and cut into large cubes
2 large onions, peeled and cut into large pieces
1 can beef broth
1 can whole tomatoes
½ cup red wine (optional)

Cut beef into large cubes. Mix flour and spices—dredge beef in flour and brown in oil in large skillet, about 10-15 minutes. Add beef broth, wine, bay leaf and 1 can water and simmer for 1 hour. Add vegetables and tomatoes and cook ½ hour more.

The Missouri mule really became famous during the first World War. Thousands were used at the front lines, hauling artillery and supplies. Their durability and toughness made a valuable contribution to the war efforts. It is very fitting that this animal is a symbol for the State, because Missourians in many ways show the same independence as these noble beasts.

"GREAT" STEAMED DUMPLINGS

FOR: Soup, Sauerkraut or Beef Stews

1½ cups flour
1½ tsp. baking powder
½ tsp. salt
1 egg
¾ cup milk

Mix flour, baking powder and salt. Add beaten egg to milk and mix together. Drop this stiff batter by teaspoon into your soups etc., one at a time.

Cover and cook on low heat 10-15 minutes.

HEARTY SHORT RIBS

3½ to 4 lbs. beef short ribs
 1 can condensed beef broth
⅓ cup flour
 3 tbsp. soft butter
 1 clove garlic finely chopped
¼ cup Mo. sherry or red wine
 1 tsp. salt
   freshly cracked pepper to
   taste
 6 peeled potatoes, quartered

Brown the short ribs in a shallow pan (such as a 9 × 13 cake pan) in a hot oven 550° for approximately 15 minutes. Drain excess fat. Lower oven temp. to 325°, add the beef broth to the ribs and cover. Bake for 2 hours or until meat is tender. During the last ½ hour, add the potatoes.

To make the gravy, melt the butter in a skillet, add the flour and slowly brown. Stir this paste into the meat juices—about 1½ cups. If not enough, add some beef broth. Add garlic and cook over medium heat until thickened. Stir in sherry and salt and pepper. Combine ribs and gravy and cook about 15 minutes. Serve ribs and potatoes with cooked and buttered carrots, green beans or vegetable of your choice.

She could out-drink, out-smoke, out-chew and out-cuss most of her fellow trappers and scouts. She is part of America's folklore. Calamity Jane is her name—born Martha Canary in Princeton, Mo. She could also out-hunt, out-ride and out-cook any of her cowboy friends. One of the earliest "superwomen"—here is her recipe for hearty short ribs, which is a favorite with the men!

TUNA BAKE

1 3 oz. can Chow Mein Noodles (Save ½ cup), put remaining in casserole and
   add:
1 can tuna, drained
1 cup cashew nuts
1 cup diced celery
¼ cup chopped onion
1 can of Cream of Mushroom
   Soup
¼ cup water or milk—mix
   well
   salt and pepper

Put remaining noodles on top.
Bake at 350°for 30–40 minutes.

Scott Joplin played a new kind of music in an old fashioned bar—The Maple Leaf Club
in Sedalia, Mo. His first big hit "Maple Leaf Rag" made him so famous that he could
spend almost all of his time composing.

PORKY PIG'S HAM LOAF

1½ lb. ground ham
1 lb. ground chuck
1½ cups bread crumbs
2 eggs, beaten
1 cup milk
¼ tsp. pepper
1 tsp. paprika
¾ tsp. dry mustard

Topping:

1 cup brown sugar
½ cup vinegar
1 tsp. dry mustard
½ cup crushed, drained
pineapple

Combine all ingredients and mix throughly. Form into loaf and cover with topping. Bake in a greased pan at 350° for 1 hour. Serves 6 to 8 people.

NOTE: a pan of water should be placed in oven to prevent loaf from getting too brown.

A little wooden desk in a schoolhouse in Marceline, Mo., has the carved initials of one of America's most beloved make-believe artists. Walt Disney grew up in this little town and was drawing at the age of 6, when he took some black tar and painted a pig on the side of the family farmhouse. The same flag flies over his schoolhouse in Marceline, as the ones which fly over Disneyland and Disneyworld.

STUFFED PEPPERS

6 green peppers
1 lb. ground chuck
¼ cup uncooked rice
3 onions
3 tsp. salt
½ tsp. freshly ground pepper
1 tsp prepared mustard
1 egg, beaten
3 tbsp. cold water
3 tbsp. butter
1 lg. can tomatoes
1 meaty beef bone
4 tbsp. brown sugar
4 tbsp. lemon juice

Place whole peppers in saucepan with water to cover. Bring to boil and remove from heat. Let sit 5 minutes, cut off tops and save. Remove seeds and ribs.

Mix beef, rice and mustard together. Grate 1 onion and add 1½ tsp. salt and ¼ tsp. pepper to beef and rice mixture. Add egg and water, stuff peppers and replace top.

Melt butter in ovenproof casserole. Peel and slice the remaining 2 onions and saute for 10 minutes, stirring occasionally. Place peppers over onions, add tomatoes, beef bone and remaining salt and pepper. Cover and bake in 325° oven for 1 hour. Add brown sugar and lemon juice and stir. Bake 30 minutes longer or until the peppers are very tender. Correct seasoning.

Would you like to visit the South as it was before the Civil War? Weston Mo., originally a bustling trade center on the Missouri River, was left behind when the river changed it's course. Though most of the population left, the town today still has the highest concentration of historic buildings in the country, and still retains it's title of "Tobacco Capitol of the West." Antebellum houses, churches and businesses date back to pre-Civil War days, when carriages and hoop skirts were the order of the day.

REAL SOUTHERN FRIED CHICKEN

1. Salt and pepper chicken pieces generously on both sides.
2. Dip chicken in milk or buttermilk, then flour. Refrigerate floured chicken for at least 2 hours.
3. Place enough oil or melted shortening in a heavy deep skillet to a depth of ½ inch. Heat over moderately high heat. Fat should sizzle when chicken is added.
4. Cook over moderately high heat until lightly browned on the bottom. Turn and brown on the other side. Chicken takes about 25 minutes. When chicken is done, remove and drain on paper towels.

Serve immediately or cover with foil and keep warm in very low oven, or chill and serve cold. Allow 2 meaty pieces or 3 bony pieces per serving.

The Civil War was truly fought in Missouri. Neighbor fought against neighbor, brother against brother, over the issue of loyalty to the North or South. More than two-thirds of Missouri's white population was of Southern Heritage, at the time of the war. It was a long and bitter struggle, and left Missouri a legacy of lawlessness and guerrilla warfare. For more than a month after Robert E. Lee surrendered, Missourians still fought the Civil War. Some say it is still being fought today or at least discussed. Missouri families will tell you with pride, on which side their ancestors fought the war.

CHICKEN CREAM GRAVY

Fried Chicken drippings
4 tbsp. flour
1 tsp. salt
¼ tsp. pepper
2 cups water or half milk, half water
1 tbsp butter

Pour off all fat except 4 tbsp. and retain brown bits in pan after frying chicken. Heat drippings, stir in flour, salt and pepper. Cook, stirring frequently, until flour is browned. Add water, cook and stir over moderate heat until smooth, thick and boiling. Just before serving, float butter on top. Makes 2 cups, 4-6 servings.

BEEF STROGANOFF

1½ lbs. sirloin beef tips (steak or tenderloin)
½ lb. fresh mushrooms, sliced
½ cup minced onions
3 tbsp. butter
1 can beef consommé (10½ oz.)
2 tbsp. catsup
1 small clove garlic
1 tsp. salt
3 tbsp. flour
1 cup sour cream

Cut meat diagonally. Saute mushrooms and onions in butter until onions are tender. Remove from skillet. In same skillet, brown meat on both sides. Set aside ⅓ cup consommé. Stir remaining consommé, catsup, garlic and salt in skillet. Cover and simmer 15 minutes.

Blend the rest of the consommé and flour and stir into skillet. Add mushrooms and onion. Heat to boiling, stirring constantly, boil 1 minute. Stir in sour cream, just before serving. (Do not boil, or sour cream will curdle.) Heat and serve on rice or noodles.

The flowering dogwood is Missouri's state tree. In late April or early May, the rolling hills of the forests are beautiful with the dogwood's white blossoms. It is as though the snow fairy wanted to remind us of winter by one last sprinkling of snow in the trees.

STUFFED CHICKEN BREASTS

3 medium sized onions, finely chopped (1½ cups)
7 tbsp. butter or margarine
½ lb. mushrooms, finely chopped (2 cups)
1 tbsp. lemon juice
½ tsp. salt
¼ tsp. pepper
1 cup soft bread crumbs (2 slices)
6 whole chicken breasts (about 12 oz. each) boned, skinned and split (12 pc.)
½ tsp. salt
⅛ tsp. pepper
½ cup white wine or apple juice
Mornay Sauce (recipe to follow)
¼ cup grated Parmesan cheese

1. Saute onions in 5 tbsp. of butter in a large skillet, until tender, about 5 minutes. Add mushrooms, lemon juice, ½ tsp. salt and ¼ tsp. pepper. Saute, stirring constantly, until liquid accumulated in skillet has evaporated, about 5 minutes. Stir in bread crumbs; cool.

2. Pound chicken breasts between sheets of wax paper to about ¼" thick. Place on work surface. Divide mushroom mixture among chicken pieces; roll up. Fasten with wooden picks.

3. Heat remaining 2 tbsp. butter in large skillet. Brown chicken breasts, half at a time, on all sides, removing to a plate as they brown. Return all to skillet; sprinkle with the remaining salt and pepper. Add wine, bring to boiling, cover, lower heat and simmer 20 minutes or just until tender.

4. While chicken cooks, prepare Mornay Sauce.

Stuffed Chicken Breasts—continued

5. Transfer chicken to 2 shallow oval baking dishes (au gratin) putting 6 pieces in each. Boil cooking liquid to reduce to ½ cup if necessary. Pour ¼ cup of liquid over chicken in each dish. Spoon Mornay Sauce over chicken, dividing evenly. Sprinkle chicken with Parmesean cheese.

6. Bake in hot oven (400°) for 15 minutes or until sauce is bubbly and top is browned. Garnish with watercress and serve with broccoli and brown or wild rice, if desired.

Much of what is thought to be bad grammar in the Ozarks is really very old English, preserved by the isolation of the mountains. Hisn, Hern and Ourn is used in the Wycliffe Bible of 1380. Chimly, a common term for chimney, was used by Sir Walter Scott in *Rob Roy*. Other words that might make city dwellers cringe, are growed, blowed, et, fit, heered and deef.

If you want to fix something that is fit for a king to "et", try this recipe for Stuffed Chicken Breasts.

MORNAY SAUCE

Melt 3 tbsp. butter or margarine in a medium-sized saucepan. Blend in 4 tbsp. flour; cook 1 minute. Gradually stir in 1 can (13¼ oz.) chicken broth. Cook, stirring constantly until sauce thickens and bubbles; cook 2 minutes. Stir in 1 cup light cream or milk. Simmer, stirring occasionally, on low heat 5 minutes. Remove from heat. Add ¼ cup shredded Swiss cheese.

TEXAS CHILI

2½ lbs. good beef arm steak or
    chuck, cut into small cubes
  1 lg. onion, chopped
  3 tbsp. salad oil
  4 cloves garlic, minced
12 oz. beer
  1 can beef broth
  1 small can tomatoes and
    green chilies
  3 tbsp. chili powder
1½ tbsp. cumin
1½ tsp. cracked black pepper
  ½ tsp. paprika
  ½ tsp. celery salt
  ½ tsp. ground hot red pepper
  ¼ tsp. sage
  ¼ tsp. ground oregano
  ¼ tsp. ground thyme
  ¼ tsp. coriander

Saute beef in oil until brown, add onions and cook about 10 minutes. Add remaining ingredients and simmer 1½-2 hours, stirring frequently.

If you want to make Missouri Chili, add 1 can of kidney beans.

Stephen Austin—who has often been called the "Father of Texas", settled that land with families from Missouri. Between the years of 1822 and 1836, almost every family in Missouri had a relative in that state. Missourians today still have a closeness for their sister state to the South.

MISSOURI HERITAGE QUILT DESIGN — NORTH CAROLINA LILY
MAKER: NANCY MILAM HOLBROOK 1813–1894

All fabrics used in this Missouri quilt (section seen above) were home-dyed at the family farm and stitched together over nearly a decade.

Vegetables and Side Dishes

SWEET POTATOES AND BLACK WALNUTS

6 large sweet potatoes
1 cup hot milk
3 tbsp. butter
½ cup brown sugar
¼ tsp. salt
½ cup black walnuts
2 tbsp. melted butter

Cook sweet potatoes in enough water to cover for about 45 minutes or until tender. Remove from heat, drain, and peel.

Mash potatoes adding hot milk, sugar, and 3 tbsp. butter and salt. Fold in ¼ cup of nuts.

Place in buttered 1½ qt. casserole. Sprinkle remaining nuts on top along with the melted butter.

Bake at 325° for 30 minutes.

Old Missourians know alot about the right planting times for different crops. All root plants such as potatoes, carrots, turnips and onions were to be planted in the dark of the moon so that they wouldn't be all "tops". Vegetables that grow above the ground were to be planted in the light of the moon. The dark of the moon is that half of the month when the moon goes from full to new moon. The light of the moon is from the new moon to full. Beans shouldn't be planted until the first call of the whipporwill is heard.

STUFFED VEGETABLES

6 zucchini, halved lengthwise
½ lbs. hot Italian sausage
¼ cup onion, chopped
1 clove garlic, minced
⅓ cup bread crumbs
¼ cup Parmesan cheese, grated
1 cup Mozzarella cheese, grated

Cook zucchini in boiling, salted water. Drain, scoop out insides leaving shell.

Mash insides, drain well.

Place shells in shallow baking dish.

Fry sausage until done. Add onion and garlic and saute until tender. Stir in mashed zucchini and bread crumbs.

Place mixture in zucchini shells. Sprinkle with cheeses.

Bake 350° for 30 minutes.

There is only one engineer in the American Hall of Fame. He is James B. Eads, the designer of the first steel truss bridge in the world. Eads' bridge in St. Louis crosses the Mississippi and was an architectural triumph of the time. It assured that St. Louis would not be left behind with the coming of the railroads.

BEAN MEDLEY

2 small cans pork & beans
1 reg. can kidney beans
1 reg. can butter beans
1 reg. can lima beans
½ lb. bacon, chopped fine
2 med. onions, chopped fine
¾ cup brown sugar
⅓ cup cider vinegar
2 tbsp. prepared mustard
   salt and pepper to taste

Brown onion and bacon together. Add brown sugar, vinegar, mustard, salt and pepper and blend. Mix with beans and bake in ovenproof casserole for 1½ hours at 350°.

John J. Pershing, the great World War I General, was born in the little town of Laclede. How lucky for America that John first saw and answered a newspaper ad for West Point Academy, which promised a free education for those who could pass the examination. His long career and great contributions make Missourians very proud of one of their "native sons". Soldiers are always eating K-rations but these are some really special beans!

112

OZARK RED CABBAGE

2 tbsp. bacon drippings
4 cups shredded red cabbage
2 cups cubed unpared apple
¼ cup brown sugar
¼ cup vinegar
1¼ tsp. salt
Dash of pepper

Heat drippings in skillet; add remaining ingredients and ¼ cup water. Cook covered over low heat; stir occasionally. For crisp cabbage, cook 15 minutes; for tender, 25-30 minutes.

The beautiful Lake of the Ozarks was created in 1931 by the building of Bagnell Dam. Twenty thousand men came from all over the country to work on the dam. Laborers worked for 35 cents an hour, rod men on survey parties made 50 cents an hour, and the survey party chiefs made $50.00 a week. They created the fourth largest man-made lake in the United States, and one of the Midwest's most popular vacation spots.

HOPPING JOHN
(This is a tradition on New Year's Eve)

1 lb. blackeyed peas	Soak peas overnight in cold water.
1½ qt. cold water	
½ lb. sliced salt pork (bacon may be substituted)	Add salt pork, tabasco sauce and salt. Cover and cook over low heat for 40 minutes.
1 tsp. tabasco sauce	
½ tsp. salt	Saute onions in bacon fat until transparent. Add to peas with rice and boiling water.
2 tbsp. bacon fat	
2 medium onions, peeled and diced	Cook until rice is tender for about 30 minutes, stirring occasionally.
1 cup uncooked rice	
1½ cup boiling water	Serves 8.
salt and pepper to taste	

Spelunking is a favorite pastime in Missouri. The exploration of caves has taken place for hundreds of years. Legend has it that gold was hidden in Missouri caves by the Spaniards. No one has found any yet. But spelunkers still have fun trying!

MINER'S FAVORITE SPINACH CASSEROLE
(Rich in Iron)

1 lg. carton small curd cottage cheese
½ cup butter, cut into small pieces
½ lb. Velveeta cheese, cut into small cubes
6 eggs, beaten
6 tbsp. flour
1 8 oz. pkg. frozen chopped spinach (defrosted & drained)

Mix all ingredients together. Pour into buttered 9" × 13" baking pan. Bake at 350° for 1 hour.

The early French explorers came to southeast Missouri looking for gold and silver, but what they found instead were large deposits of lead. Missouri leads the nation in the production of lead and southeastern Missouri is still the largest lead producing area in the world.

115

ZUCCHINI CASSEROLE

¼ cup butter
3-4 small zucchini, sliced
4 large fresh tomatoes, sliced
1 Spanish onion, sliced
1 green pepper, seeded and sliced
1 cup celery, cut into ½" diagonally sliced pieces
1 cup fresh mushrooms, sliced
3 tbsp. brown sugar
1 tsp. basil (preferably fresh)
1 tsp. oregano
½ cup chicken broth
Parmesan cheese

Saute onion and green pepper in butter just until transparent.

Add other ingredients in casserole in layers. Pour chicken broth over vegetables.

Top with Parmesan cheese and bake at 350° for 30 minutes.

Serves 4-6

The famous Dred Scott decision was made by the Supreme Court in 1857. It prevented the Missouri slave Dred Scott from winning his freedom, and was one of the events which led to the Civil War. Dred Scott did, however, eventually win his freedom.

JAZZY POTATO CASSEROLE

2 lb. bag frozen hash brown
    potatoes, thawed slightly
½ cup melted butter
1 tsp. salt
½ tsp. pepper
½ cup chopped onion
1 can cream of chicken
    soup — undiluted
1 pt. sour cream

Finish with:
2 cups crushed corn flakes
¼ cup melted butter

Place hash brown potaotes in buttered 9 × 13″ casserole.
Mix next 6 ingredients and pour over potatoes.
Top with 10 oz. grated cheese — Swiss, cheddar or a combination.

Mix corn flakes and butter and sprinkle on top of casserole. Bake at 375° for 45 minutes.
Can be made a day ahead and covered with foil and refrigerated.

Every year in June, down on the riverfront, St. Louis hosts the world's largest jazz festival. For almost twenty years, ragtime and jazz have been played until the wee hours of the morning.

CORN PUDDING

2 eggs, slightly beaten
1 small box corn meal muffin
  mix
1 18 oz. can corn, cream style
1 18 oz. can corn, whole
  kernel
1 cup sour cream
½ cup butter, melted
4 oz. Swiss cheese, shredded

Combine beaten eggs, muffin mix, corns, sour cream and butter. Put into ungreased casserole dish.

Bake at 350° for about 60 minutes. Place cheese on top and bake about 10 minutes more.

In 1914 the British bought 350,000 mules from Missouri to help win the war. West Point cadets made the mule their official mascot for their football team. Mules live 10 to 15 years longer than a horse and some say that it is out of sheer stubborness!

SPANISH RICE

Saute:

- **1 large onion, chopped**
- **1 green pepper, seeded and chopped**
- **2 cloves garlic, peeled and minced**
- **2 tbsp. butter**

Brown:

- **1 lb. ground chuck, drained**

Combine:

- **1 large can stewed tomatoes**
- **1 can tomato sauce**
- **1 tsp. worcestershire sauce**
- **½ tsp. pepper**
- **1 tsp. marjoram**
- **½ tsp. thyme**
- **1 tsp. sage**
- **1 tsp cumin**
- **½ tsp. dry mustard**
- **1 tbsp. oregano**
- **1 tbsp. chili powder**

Simmer 15 minutes. Add 1¼ cups raw rice. Lower heat and simmer until rice is cooked, about 30 minutes. Add additional liquid as necessary. Tomato juice is very good.

In the year 1821 an enterprising young man left Missouri on a trading expedition to Mexico. William Becknell has been called the "Father of the Sante Fe Trail". He was the first of thousands of Americans, who in the years 1821 to 1860, explored and conquered the western reaches of the United States.

SPOOKY WILD RICE DISH

1 cup wild rice, washed well
¼ cup chopped onion
½ cup butter
8 oz. fresh mushrooms, cleaned and sliced
1½ can beef broth
1 can water

Melt butter in skillet. Add mushrooms and onion and saute.

Add ½ can beef broth, rice and simmer 20 minutes.

Pour into oven-proof casserole and add the rest of beef broth and water. Cover and bake at 400 for 1 hour.

A strange light appears from time to time near the town of Hornet, Missouri. Long before there were roads in the area the "spook light" was scaring settlers. Some say it is the ghost of an Osage Indian chief murdered near there. Scientists have come and studied the floating light and have yet to figure out what it is. But it is spooky!

DANIEL'S FAVORITE
MAKE AHEAD MASHED POTATOES

5 lbs. boiled potatoes (pared)
2 tsp. salt in water
½ cup butter
2-3 oz. pkg. cream cheese
1 tsp. salt & pepper
½ cup sour cream

Beat this into potatoes. Stir in 2 tbsp. chopped chives. Put in large casserole, add butter & paprika on top and refrigerate one day ahead. Bake in 350° oven for 45 minutes.

Daniel Boone lived in Missouri for over 20 years. When you visit his beautiful home near Defiance, it is like stepping back in time. The blue limestone for the walls was quarried in the area and brought by oxen to the sight. They say he carved the five walnut fireplaces himself. When he died at the age of 85, loyal Kentuckians said that his body should be buried in Kentucky. Missourians let Daniel and his wife be taken back to Kentucky, but some say that it wasn't Daniel Boone's bones they took back at all, and that the old trapper and explorer still rests in his beloved Missouri.

MISSOURI HERITAGE QUILT DESIGN — **PEONY (GARDEN MAZE)**
MAKER: HARRIET BURROUGHS HUNT 1829–1919
The warm carmel color of this quilt was originally a 'fugitive' green, typical of green dyes of the 1850's and 1860's.

Sweet Nothings

SUMMER-WINTER FRUIT SURPRISE

3 cups mixed fresh fruit—
   should be mostly berries,
   but fresh peaches and necta-
   rines are very good also.
1 quart French vanilla ice
   cream (preferably home
   made)

Missouri can be a state of temperature extremes. The hottest temperature ever
recorded was 118° F at Lamar, Missouri, in July of 1936. The coldest was 40° below
zero at Warsaw, Missouri, in February of 1905. Missourians are proud of their ability
to withstand the vagaries of nature and look forward to spring and fall, which are par-
ticularly beautiful in Missouri. This dessert combines heat and cold in a wonderful
medley of tastes.

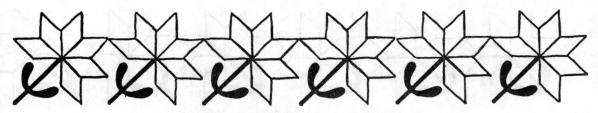

SABAYON SAUCE

6 egg yolks
⅓ cup sugar
1 cup sweet white wine

Stir constantly until thick in the top of the double boiler (*over*—not in—hot water).

Place fruit on large ovenproof platter. Spread softened ice cream over fruit and keep chilled while making Sabayon Sauce.

Pour hot Sabayon Sauce over ice cream and fruit and place for a moment under a broiler.

Serve immediately.

STRAWBERRY SHORTCAKE

1 qt. strawberries, cleaned and slightly crushed and swee- tened with ½ cup sugar
1 pt. whipping cream, whipped
1 tsp. sugar
½ tsp. vanilla, fold into whipped cream

Shortcake Recipe:

2 cups flour
½ cup butter, softened
4 tsp. baking powder
½ cup sugar
dash salt
1 cup milk

Mix dry ingredients. Cut in butter, add milk. Do not overmix. Pour into buttered and floured 8" cake pan.

Bake at 450° for 15 to 18 minutes or until a tooth- pick inserted in the center of cake comes out clean. Cut into wedges while warm, split cake, top with berries and cake, more berries and sweetened whipped cream.

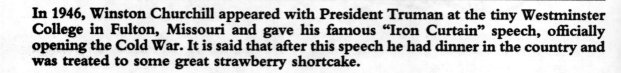

In 1946, Winston Churchill appeared with President Truman at the tiny Westminster College in Fulton, Missouri and gave his famous "Iron Curtain" speech, officially opening the Cold War. It is said that after this speech he had dinner in the country and was treated to some great strawberry shortcake.

BLACKBERRY COBBLER

½ cup butter, softened
1 cup flour
1 to 2 cups sugar
1 cup milk
2 tsp. baking powder
1 qt. fresh blackberries, cleaned
1 pt. half and half

Cut flour into butter, add 1 cup sugar, milk and baking powder. Mix until just blended.

Pour into buttered 8″ square pan.

Sprinkle ¾ to 1 cup sugar over berries. Stir gently.

Pour berries into center of pan. Bake at 350° for 35 to 40 minutes.

Serve warm, with light cream in bowls.

Springfield, Missouri was founded by farmers and is known as the berry capital of the nation. It is also known as the Queen City of the Ozarks, perhaps because two major highways lead to Springfield and farther into the resort land of the Ozarks.

DRIED APPLE STACKING CAKE

1 cup sugar
1 cup butter, softened
1 cup sorghum molasses
¼ cup buttermilk
1 egg
2 tsp. soda dissolved in 1 tbsp. vinegar
½ tsp. salt
1 tsp. cinnamon
½ tsp. ginger
¼ tsp. nutmeg
4 cups flour

Filling:
4 cups dried apples
¼ cup cream
½ to ¾ cup sugar

Cream together butter and sugar. Add molasses, egg and buttermilk and mix well.

Stir in dry ingredients along with the vinegar, soda mixture.

Divide dough into 6 parts. Press 1 part into greased 8″ cake pan. Repeat with rest of dough.

Bake at 350° for 15-20 minutes or until slightly browned.

Remove from pans while warm and set aside to cool.

Put dried apples in saucepan with 2 cups water. Cook over low heat until soft.

Drain apples and mash together with cream to make a smooth paste.

Spread apple mixture between cake layers. Leave top layer of cake plain but sprinkle with confectioners sugar.

Refrigerate cake for 12 hours minimum before serving.

On August 10, 1821 Missouri was admitted to the Union as the 24th state. Under the "Missouri Compromise" Act, Congress admitted Missouri as a slave state, but prohibited slavery west and north of the state.

GLISTENING COCONUT CREAM PIE

1 baked pie shell
2 egg yolks, slightly beaten
1 cup sugar
2 cups milk
2½ tbsp. corn starch
  dash salt
1 cup coconut + ¼ cup

Meringue:

2 egg whites
¼ tsp. cream of tartar
¼ cup sugar

Combine milk, sugar, egg yolks, and salt in saucepan. Bring to boil, stirring constantly. Thicken with cornstarch mixed with 3 tbsp. water. Cook and stir until smooth. Remove from heat.

Stir in coconut and pour into baked pie shell. Top with meringue.

Beat egg whites until frothy. Add sugar slowly and beat until stiff. Place on top of pie with coconut. Brown in hot oven (400°) until browned.

Kansas City has been called the "City of Fountains." They are everywhere, surprising visitors with their beauty and musical motion. Each year a new fountain is added and it is said that Kansas City has more fountains than any other city in the world except Rome.

HARRY'S FAVORITE LEMON PIE

½ cup graham cracker crumbs
3 egg whites
½ cup sugar
3 egg yolks
1 cup whipping cream
2 to 3 tsp. grated lemon rind
¼ to ⅓ cup lemon juice

Sprinkle half of the crumbs in a well buttered 9" pie pan.

Beat egg whites until frothy. Gradually add sugar. Beat until stiff and glossy.

Beat egg yolks until thick and lemon-colored. Fold into egg white mixture.

Mix cream, lemon rind and juice and beat until stiff. Fold into egg mixture.

Pour into crumb lined pie pan. Sprinkle rest of crumbs on top.

Freeze to desired consistency. Serves 7-8.

LEMON

The frame cottage which was the birthplace of our 33rd President has been lovingly restored. Harry S. Truman, son of a mule trader, was born in the back bedroom of this little house in Lamar, Missouri. A stone tablet in the yard quotes the President's words from his first address to the U. S. Congress in 1945, "I ask only to be a good and faithful servant to my Lord and my people."

HOMEMADE PEACH ICE CREAM

3 eggs
1½ qt. half and half (6 cups)
1 qt. whipping cream
¼ tsp. salt
3 tbsp. vanilla
3 cups sugar (if peaches are tart, add ½ to 1 cup more sugar)
4-5 cups peeled peaches, sliced and slightly mashed

Beat eggs in large bowl, add 1 qt. of half & half and beat. Add salt, vanilla and 3 cups sugar. Stir and pour into freezer container. Add remaining half & half, whipping cream and fruit. Taste and add more sugar if necessary. Freezing lessens the sugar taste. Freeze according to manufacturer's directions. Makes 1 gallon.

Can be frozen, but will probably be eaten before then.

Feel like having fun? Visit "World's of Fun", Kansas City's Theme park on the city's outskirts. Five different international theme areas and 110 different rides keep everyone busy. There are also music and dance reviews, animal acts, super star concerts, restaurants and shops. When you're finished, make some homemade ice cream and relax and talk about the day's activities.

WINE COUNTRY STRAWBERRY PIE

1½ qt. fresh strawberries
⅔ cup water
1 cup sugar
3 tbsp. cornstarch
⅓ cup water
6 oz. cream cheese
½ pt. whipping cream
1 baked pie shell

Clean berries, reserving ½ cup. Take 1 cup berries and ⅔ cup water and simmer for 3 minutes.

Blend sugar, cornstarch and ⅓ cup water; add to boiling mixture. Boil 1 minute and cool.

Spread softened cream cheese over pie crust and place berries, stem side down on cream cheese. Pour cooked strawberry mixture over pie and refrigerate until firm. Top with extra berries and sweetened whipped cream.

You can tour Missouri's wine country and if ambitious enough, visit the 32 winerys which make up Missouri's wine industry. Most are family owned and will offer tours and tastings, but it is a good idea to call ahead. Enjoy the scenery and the history and perhaps even a bed and breakfast in a country cottage.

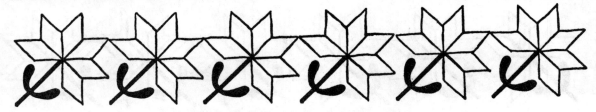

PERSIMMON PUDDING

2 cups buttermilk
2 cups ripe persimmon pulp
1 cup sugar
1 egg
1 tbsp. butter
½ tsp. baking powder
½ tsp. soda
¼ tsp. cloves
¼ tsp. nutmeg
½ tsp. allspice
1 tsp. cinnamon
1 cup flour

Topping:
1 pt. whipping cream,
   whipped and sweetened with
1 tbsp. sugar

Mix buttermilk with ripe persimmon pulp. Blend in a blender. Put in large bowl and add sugar, egg, butter, baking powder, soda and spices. Add flour and mix.

Pour into buttered casserole. Bake at 350° for about 45 minutes or until knife inserted in center comes out clean.

Pudding will fall when cool. Cut into squares and serve with whipped cream.

In the spring of 1804, twelve Osage chiefs left St. Louis to visit President Jefferson. Among them was White Hair, a chieftain who acquired his name from a grey wig, which to his surprise, came off in his hand when attempting to scalp the victim. He always wore it afterward as a charm.

FUNNEL CAKES

2 eggs, beaten
2 cups sifted flour
½ tsp. salt
1½ cups milk
1 tsp. baking powder
½ tsp. vanilla
   salad oil

Beat eggs and milk together. Add vanilla. Sift dry ingredients and add to egg mixture. Beat until smooth.

Heat oil (about 3 cups) to 360°. Pour ¼ cup batter through a small funnel into oil. As you pour batter, make a lacy circle.

Fry a minute on each side or until golden brown. Remove from fat and drain on paper towels. Sprinkle with powdered sugar and serve with warm honey

Walk through Soulard Market in St. Louis and one might believe that time's been turned back. Soulard becomes a bustling European open-air market, complete with live chickens and ducks, noisy vendors hawking fresh fruits and vegetables, and the fish catch of the day glistening on ice. The Soulard area around the market is a National Historic District. Take the whole family and enjoy some funnel cakes made right before your eyes, or make your own with this easy recipe.

DUTCH APPLE PIE IN A SACK
(It really works!)

1 unbaked 9″ pastry shell
⅔ cup sugar
2 tbsp. flour
8-10 apples, pared and sliced
6 tbsp. butter
½ cup brown sugar
1 cup flour
   salt

Heat oven to 425°.

Shake sugar, spice, flour and apples in a sack. Arrange in a pie crust.

Combine butter, brown sugar, flour and a pinch of salt to make crumb topping.

Sprinkle on apple mixture. Bake in a sealed brown paper sack for 1 hour. 6–8 servings.

Before there were roads or signposts in the Ozark hills, Indians had their own way of finding things. They were called Thong Trees. Young saplings were tied with leather thongs in an arrow position and left to grow that way. They pointed the way to water, salt, caves and burial grounds and can still be seen today.

PERFECT PIE CRUST

4 cups unsifted flour
2 tsp. salt
1 tbsp. sugar
1¾ cup good quality solid
   vegetable shortening
½ cup cold water
1 large egg
1 tbsp. white vinegar

Sift flour, salt and sugar together in large mixing bowl. Cut in shortening until mixture resembles cornmeal. Beat egg and add to water and vinegar. Slowly add to flour, shortening mixture. Blend just until mixture clings together.

Chill 30 minutes. Divide dough in half. Roll out on lightly floured board to ⅛ inch thickness. Fill with desired fruit or custard filling and bake.

BUTTER PIE CRUST

2¼ cup all-purpose flour
1 tsp. salt
⅔ cup solid vegetable shortening, chilled
5 tbsp. salted butter, cut into
   small pieces
7 tbsp. water

Sift flour and salt together in large mixing bowl. Cut in shortening and butter until mixture resembles cornmeal.

Sprinkle water over mixture. Blend gently until all ingredients are moistened and dough holds together.

Divide dough into two portions. Chill dough.

Place one portion on floured surface, roll to ⅛" thickness using a light hand.

Place in pie pan, fill with desired filling and roll out second portion and top.

Note: If baking an unfilled pie crust bake at 425° for 20 to 25 minutes, pricking with fork.

Trail of Tears State Park is a sad memorial to the Cherokee Indian Tribe. The Indians were moving to a new home in Oklahoma from Appalachia when winter weather struck them with surprising severity. Even though Missourians tried to help by providing clothing and food, many died. The park has 3,000 acres of rolling land which is a fitting tribute to a great people.

KINDER CARAMEL APPLES

6 cups sugar
4 cups dark Karo syrup
1 cup whipping cream
⅓ cup water
2 cans evaporated milk

Mix together and bring to boil

Add 2 cans evaporated milk. Boil 4-5 minutes or to 240°. Do not stop boiling when adding milk.

Dip the apples in caramel and put on sugared trays.

Note: Use about 50 small apples.

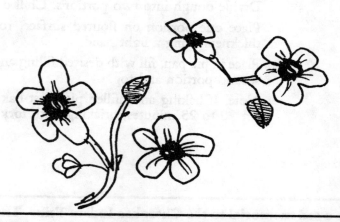

She has been called the "Mother of Kindergarten". Susan Elizabeth Blow became deeply interested in early education and was instrumental in establishing the first public school kindergarten in 1873 in Missouri. Her portrait can be seen in the State Capitol.

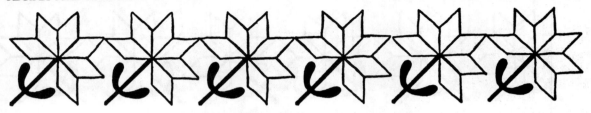

SWEET POTATO PIE

2 cups mashed, cooked sweet potatoes
4 eggs
½ cup sugar
⅔ cup milk
2 tbsp. honey
¼ tsp. salt
2 tbsp. applejack or brandy
⅓ cup orange juice
½ tsp. nutmeg
unbaked pie shell

Beat eggs until frothy. Add sugar and sweet potatoes beating until smooth.

Beat in rest of ingredients.

Pour into an unbaked pie shell and bake at 450° for 10 minutes. Reduce heat to 350° and bake 30 minutes longer or until knife inserted in center comes out clean.

Top with:
1 cup whipping cream, whipped
2 tsp. sugar
1 tbsp. grated orange rind
1 tbsp. applejack (optional)

Beat cream until stiff, then add sugar, orange rind and applejack.

The people of Missouri have always wanted to hear the news truthfully. The world's first school of Journalism was started at the University of Missouri in Columbia in 1908.

CARAMEL TOPPED APPLE CAKE

1¼ cup salad oil
2 cups sugar
3 eggs
1 tsp. vanilla
3 cups raw apples, chopped
3 cups cake flour, sifted
1 tsp. salt
1 tsp. soda
1 cup nuts, chopped

Do not use mixer. Beat eggs, add sugar, oil and vanilla. Stir in 3 cups apples.

Sift and measure 3 cups cake flour with salt and soda.

Mix nuts in flour. Add apple batter to flour and nut mixture. Mix well.

Bake in tube pan or sheet pan at 325° for about 1 hour 5 minutes.

Cool before adding topping.

Topping: (for sheet cake double topping recipe)

½ stick margarine
¼ cup evaporated milk
1 cup light brown sugar

Combine above and bring to a boil. For thicker mixture cook longer and whip until thick and creamy.

Cool and spread on cake.

Freezes well!

You can hear some tall tales told at the Storytelling Festival held on the Riverfront in St. Louis. All kinds of people participate, from teachers to professional storytellers to just an interested bystander. Practice your storytelling technique while you enjoy a piece of Caramel Topped Apple Cake.

CELEBRATION CHEESE CAKE

1 pkg. graham crackers, crushed—may be done in blender (about 8 large crackers)
2 tbsp. sugar
½ cup butter
1 lb. cream cheese
⅔ cup sugar
½ tsp. almond extract
3 eggs
1 cup sour cream
3 tsp. sugar
1 tsp. vanilla

Melt butter, mix with cracker crumbs and sugar. Press into 10″ pie pan.

Blend cream cheese, eggs, ⅔ cup sugar and almond extract. Pour into prepared pie shell. Bake approximately 40 min. at 350°.

Remove from oven and cool until flat. Mix together sour cream, sugar and vanilla and spread on cheese cake. Bake again for 10 minutes at 350°.

Kansas City is the home of Hallmark Cards, whose greetings for every kind of family celebration have been mailed to almost every family in the U. S. Their slogan, "when you care enough to send the very best", might be changed in the cooking of this recipe to "when you care enough to cook the very best."

GREEK EASTER COOKIES

5 cups all purpose flour
10 eggs
1 lb. butter—at room temperature
2½ cups sugar
5 tsp. baking powder
1 tsp. vanilla
1 orange peel finely shredded

Beat softened butter for 10 minutes with mixer, add eggs 1 at a time and beat for 15 minutes more. Add sugar and continue to beat for about 15 minutes or until sugar is mixed thoroughly in and has melted.

Mix baking powder with flour and add to butter mixture at intervals with mixer set on blend. Add vanilla and orange peel.

Grease a cookie sheet and drop by teaspoonful in an oblong shape. Bake at 325° for 10-15 minutes.

Cookies should first be placed on bottom rack of oven and when cookies start to brown on bottom, move pan to top rack.

Makes enough for a large family and many friends—or about 10 dozen.

Every year in Forest Park in St. Louis, Missourians from 35 different nationalities gather together. The occasion is the annual International Festival, showcasing the music, dress, foods and crafts from many different lands.

BLACK WALNUT BUNDT CAKE

1 white cake mix
1 pkg. vanilla pudding mix
4 eggs
½ cup water
½ cup orange juice
½ cup salad oil
2 caps vanilla extract
¾ cup finely chopped black walnuts + ¼ cup for frosting

Mix all ingredients in a large bowl and beat on medium speed for 4 minutes.

Greese and flour bundt pan or tube cake pan. Pour into pan and bake at 350° for 60–65 minutes.

If desired, frost with a simple powdered sugar frosting made by combining about 1½ cups powdered sugar, 3 tbsp. soft butter or margarine, ½ tsp. vanilla and enough milk or cream to desired consistency. Sprinkle top of of cake with chopped black walnuts.

walnut

Warsaw, Missouri is the gunstock capital of the world. Walnut trees abound in the area and provide the wood for the beautiful gunstocks. Almost 90% of the worlds gunstocks are produced here. Before the wood becomes a finished product, it is dried in silos for 6 months or longer, carved, sanded and finished with pride. Some finished guns have brought as much as $7,500.00 on special order.

EASY GRAND MARNIER SOUFFLE

Everyone thinks that souffles are too hard to make, but they are really easy and also very good.

2 cups milk
¾ cup sugar
⅓ cup flour
2 oz. butter
5 egg yolks
7 egg whites
2 oz. Grand Marnier

SOUFFLE

Beat egg whites until stiff. Heat milk, add sugar and stir and bring to a boil. Melt butter and mix with flour. Mix butter, flour mixture with milk and stir until it is creamy and slightly thickened.

Remove from heat, add Grand Marnier. Beat egg yolks until lemon in color and add to mixture continually stirring. Gently fold in beaten egg whites.

Pour into buttered, sugared souffle mold or 1½ quart casserole. Bake in 400° oven for 20 to 25 minutes.

DO NOT OPEN OVEN DOOR WHILE BAKING.

She arrived in St. Louis in the heat of the summer in 1764. The only white woman in the area, she must not have had an easy time. Known for her gentle ways, her charity and graciousness, Marie Theresa Choteau has been called the "Mother of St. Louis."

BELLE'S BREAD PUDDING

2 cups milk
⅓ cup butter
4 cups coarse breadcrumbs
½ cup plus 1 tbsp. sugar
2 eggs, slightly beaten
¼ tsp. salt
½ cup raisins
1 tsp. cinnamon
¼ tsp. nutmeg
1 tsp. vanilla
¾ cup drained, crushed
pineapple
½ cup coconut

Scald milk and remove from heat. Melt butter in milk and then pour over bread crumbs. Add rest of ingredients.

Pour into buttered baking dish and bake at 350° for 40 to 45 minutes or until a knife comes out clean.

Serve with light cream or a rich custard sauce, or Bourbon Sauce.

They say that she was a "lady outlaw". She wore a long black velvet gown, a white Stetson hat with an ostrich plume in the band, black leather gloves and boots and two sixshooters. Her name was Belle Starr and she came from an aristocratic southern family from Carthage, Missouri. How she came to ride with the Younger Gang, and was known as a female Robin Hood is another story for another day, but between her jaunts, she liked to whip together some good bread pudding for the boys.

Belle's Bread Pudding—continued

Bourbon Sauce

- **3 tbsp. butter**
- **1 cup firmly packed brown sugar (light brown)**
- **⅛ tsp. salt**
- **2 tbsp. bourbon**
- **1 cup whipping cream**

Brown butter in skillet over medium heat, stir in brown sugar using a wooden spoon. Cook mixture over low heat, stirring frequently, until sugar dissolves. Add bourbon and whipping cream, stirring well. Continue cooking until sauce thickens. Serve sauce over warm pudding.

Yield: about 1½ cups.

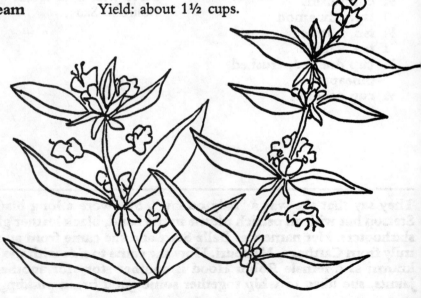

SOUTHERN BANANA PUDDING
(A Classic Favorite)

1 pkg. vanilla pudding mix
  (not instant)
2 egg yolks, slightly beaten
2½ cups milk
25 vanilla wafers
3 large bananas
2 egg whites
  dash of salt
¼ cup sugar

Combine pudding mix, egg yolks and milk in saucepan. Cook and stir over medium heat until mixture comes to a full boil. Remove from heat. Arrange layer of vanilla wafers on bottom and sides of a 1½ qt. baking dish. Add a layer of banana slices and then pudding. Continue layering, ending with pudding.

Beat egg whites with salt until foamy. Gradually beat in sugar and continue beating until mixture forms stiff peaks. Spoon onto pudding, sealing edges well.

Beat at 425° for 5 to 10 minutes, until lightly browned. Serve warm or chilled. Serves 8.

Silver Dollar City, near Branson, Mo. was built on the site of an old Ozark mining town. It is a reconstruction of an Ozark village of the 1880s. Old time crafts are demonstrated by costumed craftsmen. Wood carving, glass blowings, weaving, pottery, and candy making are just a few of the 28 crafts demonstrated year round in the town. Entertainment—country style is around every corner and for young and old to enjoy.

FRENCH CHOCOLATE SILK PIE

½ cup butter or margarine
¾ cup sugar
1 sq. unsweetened chocolate, melted
1 tsp. vanilla
2 eggs
1 baked pastry shell

Cream butter and sugar; add melted chocolate and vanilla. Add 1 egg and beat 5 minutes at high speed. Add second egg and beat 5 minutes more. Pour into baked pie shell and refrigerate. When ready to serve, top with whipped cream. May add finely chopped nuts and shaved chocolate on top.

Pierre LaClede Liquest, better known as Pierre LaClede, founded the city of St. Louis, in the spring of 1764. Together with his young stepson August Chouteau, they developed a trading post which LaClede named in honor of Louis IX, patron saint of the reigning Louis XV. As he stood on the banks of the great Mississippi, he turned to his young companion and said, "It may become one of the finest cities in America". In honor of our French founder, we give you this recipe for French Chocolate Silk Pie, of which we are sure he would have asked to have a second piece!

APPLE TORTE

¾ cup sugar
1 egg
1 tsp. vanilla
½ tsp. salt
1 tsp. baking powder
½ cup flour
1 cup chopped raw apples
½ cup chopped walnuts or almonds

Mix together sugar, egg, vanilla, and salt. In separate bowl, sift flour and baking powder together, then slowly add to sugar mixture. Fold in apples and nuts. Pour into a greased 9" pie pan. Bake at 350° until golden and crusted (about 25 minutes).

This comes out crisp, aromatic and wonderful. Serve warm or cold, with whipped cream or ice cream, any way it's delightful!

In 1816, James Hart Stark, a young Kentucky pioneer, settled with his family in Missouri. He brought with him switches of apple trees from his father's farm. After grafting the branches to the local wild crab apple trees, he succeeded in growing the first cultivated fruit west of the Mississippi. Stark Nursery is today one of the largest in the world and the oldest in America. It was here that the popular Red and Golden Delicious apples were first developed. Stark apples are good baking apples, especially good in this recipe for apple torte.

PEANUT BARS

3 cups flour, sifted
5 tsp. baking powder
1 tsp. salt
2 cups sugar
1 tbsp. grated orange rind
¾ cup shortening
4 eggs
1 cup milk

Frosting:
½ cup butter
2½ cups powdered sugar
1 tsp. orange juice

Beat sugar and shortening well. Add eggs, one at a time, and beat well after each egg. Alternately add dry ingredients with milk. Beat one minute.

Pour into well greased and floured 9 × 13 pan. Bake 30–35 minutes at 350°.

When cake has cooled, cut into squares and frost with icing made from:

Stir until smooth, adding enough light cream until icing is quite thin. Spread on squares of cake then roll in finely chopped salted peanuts.

The barefoot boy, who was the son of a slave, had dreams for his fellow man far beyond the boundaries of the state of Missouri. George Washington Carver, born in the little town of Diamond, Mo., was a brilliant scientist, teacher and humanitarian who is perhaps best remembered for his experiments with the humble peanut plant.

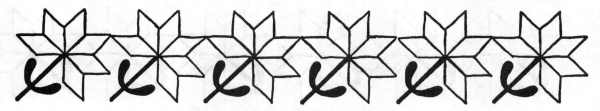

MOUND BARS

2 cups crushed graham crackers **½ cup butter, melted** **¼ cup sugar**	Mix and press into a 9" x 13" pan. Bake 10 minutes at 350°.
1 package angel flake coconut **1 can sweetened condensed milk**	Mix together and pour on crust and bake 15 minutes more.
1 cup butterscotch chips **1 cup chocolate chips**	Mix chips and place in top of double boiler or microwave oven. Melt over hot water. Do not let water boil. Spread on top of bars.

The original inhabitants of Missouri were people of Indian ancestry. Missouri has always been a desirable place to live and archaeological research has shown people living in Missouri for more than 10,000 years. Various cultures have flowered and then disappeared, but one of the more interesting was that of the Mississippi Period. The people of this period built mounds on which were built temples and houses of the chiefs and priests. St. Louis and Cahokia, across the river in Illinois seem to have been part of a large city with more than 25,000 people. St. Louis was often called "Mound City" in early years.

GRANDMA'S BUTTER CRISPS

Sift:

2¼ cups sifted flour
1 cup sifted confectioner's sugar
½ tsp. salt

Cut in:

½ cup soft butter and
½ cup margarine until mixture resembles coarse meal.

Beat:

1 egg until light

Sprinkle:

2 tbsp. of the beaten egg and
2 tsp. vanilla over mixture

Blend well and form into a ball. Dough may be chilled.

Roll out — ⅓ at a time to a thickness of ⅛".

Cut out with cookie cutter. Place on ungreased cookie sheets. Brush with remaining egg. Sprinkle with plain or colored sugar. Bake at 375° for 5 to 8 minutes.

Missouri — sometimes pronounced Missooree and sometimes pronounced Missourah, has strong supporters for both pronunciations. The northern half of the state usually goes with ee and the southern half with ah, but politically ambitious public figures generally use whichever is popular, depending on where they are speaking! However you want to say it, these are some of the best cookies to be found in Missouri, or is it Missourah?

MISSISSIPPI MUD PIE

20 Oreo Cookies, crushed
½ cup butter, melted
1 qt. Coffee Ice Cream,
   softened
1 small jar Hot Fudge
   Topping
1 cup Dry Roasted Salted
   Peanuts
   Whipped Cream

Mix crushed cookies and butter. Press into a greased 9" pie pan and chill. Spread softened ice cream into crust and freeze. Spread hot fudge topping over ice cream, add the peanuts and freeze. Top with a small amount of whipped cream, if desired. Let pie sit out of freezer for about 10 minutes before cutting. Makes 8 servings.

Missouri is a state of rivers bordered by the great Mississippi on the east and the Missouri on the west. These two rivers provide 1,000 miles of navigable waterways within the state, and connect river traffic from Minnesota to Louisiana.

SWEET KEWPIE COMPOTE

Delicious with sweetened whipped cream flavored with kirsch or vanilla.

4 cups sliced fresh or frozen
  rhubarb (1 lb.)
2 cups sugar
⅛ tsp. salt
2 cups fresh or thawed frozen
  strawberries, hulled and
  halved (1 pt.)
2 medium oranges, peeled,
  sliced and halved (optional)

In large stainless-steel or enamelware skillet, mix rhubarb, sugar and salt. Cover and cook over very low heat without stirring 20-25 minutes or until rhubarb is tender, shaking skillet occasionally. Cool, stir in strawberries and oranges. Chill in serving dish. Makes 4-6 servings.

Remember Kewpie Dolls, those roly poly cherubs? They were first designed by Rose O'Neill, a gifted Missouri artist. They became so popular in the early 1900s, that over 21 factories in Germany were making them. Though she traveled and lived many places in the U. S. and abroad, she always returned to her Ozark home in Taney County. Bonniebrook was her home and her inspiration for her many novels and poems. She called it "the enchanted tangle", and said "her heart was tangled in it for good".

BANANA CAKE

⅔ cup soft shortening
1½ cups sugar
2 large eggs
2½ cups sifted cake flour
1¼ tsp. baking powder
1¼ tsp. soda
1 tsp. salt
1¼ cups mashed ripe bananas
(about 3–4)
⅔ cup buttermilk
⅔ cup chopped walnuts

Cream shortening and sugar, add eggs and beat until fluffy. Sift together dry ingredients, add alternately with buttermilk and bananas. Beat until smooth with mixer. Mix nuts in with flour.

Pour batter into 2, 8" round pans or 1, 9" × 13" pan, which has been greased and floured. Bake 45-50 minutes at 350°. Cool before frosting.

Frosting:

6 tbsp. brown sugar
4 tbsp. light cream (Half and Half)
2 tbsp. butter
1 cup powdered sugar (approx.)

Combine first 3 ingredients in a small kettle and bring to a boil. Boil for 1 minute, remove from heat, add powdered sugar and beat. Frost cake immediately.

There was an old man who was known as "The Hound Tuner of Calloway". He rode around Calloway County on a decrepit old horse with his tuning fork and tested the vocal chords of the county's hound dogs. He must have been kept busy, because Calloway is said to have had more hounds than people at one time.

Sometimes, when he stopped at a farmhouse he was offered a piece of wonderful Banana Cake.

LEMON BARS

1½ cups confectioner's sugar
1¾ cups margarine
2½ cups flour
1¼ cups granulated sugar
1 tbsp. baking powder
5 eggs, beaten
1 cup lemon juice
2½ cups coconut

Cream together confectioner's sugar and margarine thoroughly. When creamy, add flour and mix well. Pack evenly in 13″ × 18″ pan or two 9″ × 13″ pans. Bake in 350° oven for 15 minutes. Do not overbake. Mix together granulated sugar and baking powder, add to beaten eggs; mix well. Stir in 1 cup lemon juice, then coconut. Be sure batter is blended. Pour batter over baked crust. Bake 350° for 20-25 min. or until done. Cool, dribble lemon frosting over all.

Lemon Frosting:

2 cups confectioner's sugar
¼ cup butter, softened
½ lemon juice

Beat together confectioner's sugar, butter and lemon juice until smooth.

Old Jim was just a hunting dog. A good hunting dog, you understand, but just a dog, or was he? Down in Sedalia, people still talk about what Jim could do. This was back in the 1930's and it seems the old dog could understand perfectly what people said to him. He could pick out people's cars by being told the license numbers, the lady in the red raincoat, the hickory tree and even his master's brand of cigar, from the corner drugstore. Most amazing of all, he picked the winner of the Kentucky Derby for seven years in a row. He earned the name, Wonder Dog, and he really deserved it.

If Jim were human he would really have enjoyed these Lemon Bars.

OLYMPIC CHOCOLATE KISSES

2- 1 lb. pkg. Hershey sweet
    chocolate bars
  2 squares of bitter chocolate
  1 lb. dates cut into small
    pieces
½ lb. raisins, cut
  5 cups corn flakes
  1 cup pecan pieces

Melt chocolate in top of double boiler. Pour over corn flakes, dates, raisins and nuts, and mix until flakes are coated. Drop by tbsp. onto wax paper and let stand until firm.

The first Olympic marathon in the Western Hemisphere occurred in St. Louis on August 30, 1904. Thirty-one runners began the race at Francis Field at Washinton University. Runners had to contend with 94° temperatures, bad roads, clouds of dust produced by thoughtless motorists and biting dogs. Only fourteen runners completed the race.

SOUR CREAM RAISIN PIE

1 9″ baked pie shell
1 cup raisins
1 cup sour cream
1 cup sugar
2 eggs
1 3 oz. pkg. cream cheese
½ cup powdered sugar
1 cup whipping cream
(whipped)
1 tsp. cinnamon
½ tsp. cloves
1 tbsp. butter
¼ tsp. salt

Cook raisins, sour cream, eggs and spices. Bring to a boil and cook until thickened, stirring constantly. Cool completely.

Blend cream cheese, powdered sugar and whipping cream.

Spread ½ of this mixture into pie shell, add cooled raisin mixture and then other ½ of cream cheese mixture. Chill and garnish, if desired with sweetened whipped cream.

Country Club Plaza in Kansas City, is the United States oldest shopping center. Designed in 1922, by J. C. Nichols, it's Spanish style architecture and many specialty shops makes it a unique place to visit. After shopping, a piece of Sour Cream Raisin Pie tastes really good!

MATRIMONIAL DATE BARS

1½ cups flour
1½ cups oatmeal
¼ tsp. salt
1 tsp. baking powder
½ tsp. baking soda
1 cup butter
1 cup brown sugar

Filling:

½ lb. dates (cut up)
½ cup water
2 tbsp. brown sugar
1 tsp. lemon juice

Mix dry ingredients, cut in butter. Set aside.

Cook filling mixture over low heat stirring constantly until thickened, about 10 minutes.

Place ½ of crumb mixture in greased and floured 13" × 9" oblong pan. Press and flatten with hands to cover bottom of pan. Spread with cooled filling. Cover with remaining crumb mixture, patting lightly. Bake until lightly browned, 400° for 25–30 minutes. While still warm, cut into bars.

Old traditions still linger on in the Ozark hills. On May 1st, at sun-up, some young ladies still wash their faces with dew, hoping to marry the man they love the most.

ANGEL PIE

3 egg whites
1 cup sugar
¾ tsp. lemon juice or vinegar
1 pint whipping cream

Beat egg white until stiff (holds a point). Gradually beat in ½ cup sugar, then alternately add juice or vinegar with remaining ½ cup sugar. Beat mixture until very stiff and glossy.

Line one 9″ pie plate with brown paper. Bake until delicately browned and crusty. Bake at 275° for 60 minutes. Cool, remove paper and fill with whipped cream (Whip 1 cup whipping cream until stiff. Spread half of it over Meringue Shell. Save remaining half.) Spread with cooled lemon custard filling. Top with remaining whipped cream. Chill about 12 hours before serving.

Lemon Custard Filling:
4 egg yolks
½ cup sugar
4 tbsp. lemon juice
2 tbsp. grated lemon rind

Cook over hot water, stirring constantly until thick (5–8 minutes.) Cool.

Many natural formations in the Ozarks were named by the Scotch-Irish settlers, from the Appalachian highlands. They seem to have been preoccupied with the Devil, because there are Devil backbones, hollows, tables, racetracks, dens and toll gates. No less than 90 natural features refer to that great tempter and may others to Hell. This is in contrast to the southwestern United States, where angels and Heaven predominate. You might even be tempted by this recipe for Angel Pie.

TOM SAWYER'S PRALINES

1 cup sugar
½ cup whipping cream, heavy
3 tbsp. dark corn syrup
1/16 tsp. baking soda
1/16 tsp. salt
1 or 2 cups pecan halves
½ tsp. vanilla

In heavy 2 qt. pan cook over medium heat sugar, cream, syrup, soda and salt. Stir until sugar dissolves.

Bring to a boil. Boil withour stirring to 234° (soft ball stage).

Remove from heat. Add pecan halves and vanilla.

Drop by teaspoonfuls on lightly buttered baking sheet or wax paper. Let stand until cool and set.

Pecan

Visit Hannibal, Missouri over the 4th of July and take part in "Tom Sawyer Days". Some of the activities are frog jumping contests, river raft races and fence painting contests.

EASY FUDGE

4½ cups granulated sugar
⅔ cup butter (1⅓ sticks)
1 large can evaporated milk
3 small packages chocolate bits
1 jar marshmallow cream
1 cup chopped nuts (optional)

Mix and bring to full boil. Boil 8 minutes.

Add 3 small packages of chocolate bits and 1 jar marshmallow cream. Add chopped nuts if desired.

Pour into buttered pan. Cool and cut in squares.

Yields about 5 pounds.

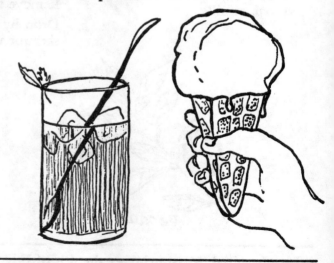

The St. Louis World's Fair of 1904 was remarkable in many ways. Three all-American foods were invented at the Fair. The hot dog, the ice cream cone and iced tea.

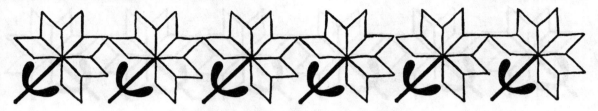

ENGLISH TOFFEE

1 pound *butter*
1 pound white sugar
2 Hershey candy bars
1 cup walnuts

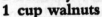

Boil to 290°.

Spread in buttered jelly roll pan and cover with two Hershey candy bars.

Then add ground nuts on top of Hershey bars which have been spread over toffee and cool in refrigerator.

When cold, turn pan upside down and candy will fall out. Crack into bite size pieces.

Ice Cream and waffles were being sold side by side in booths at the 1904 World's Fair. The ice cream man ran out of cups for his ice cream, so he took a warm waffle and made a cone for the ice cream.

SUGARED NUTS

3 cups nuts (peanuts, whole almonds, pecan halves, walnuts or a mix of your favorite nuts)
1 cup sugar
½ cup water

In 12″ skillet over medium heat, bring nuts, sugar and water to a boil.

Cook stirring occasionally, until syrup mixture has carmelized, and the nuts are well coated. About 12 to 15 minutes. The bottom of the skillet should appear dry.

Immediately spread coated nuts onto buttered baking sheet.

Bake in 300° oven for 10 minutes, stir. Bake 10 minutes longer, stir again.

Cool on rack. Store in airtight container. Makes 4 cups or about ¼ pound.

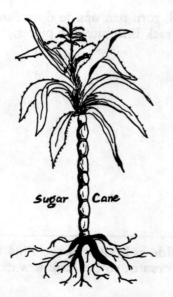

Sugar Cane

PEANUT BRITTLE

2 cups white sugar
¼ cup water
¼ cup vinegar
½ cup Karo syrup (Blue Label)
¼ pound *butter*
1 tsp. vanilla
1 lb. Spanish peanuts

Cook first five ingredients to hard crack stage.

Add vanilla and peanuts and pour into large flat buttered pan.

When cold, chop into pieces.

A sausage peddler at the World's Fair was an enterprising young man. He gave his customers disposable gloves to eat his hot sausage with. But when the gloves became a problem, he talked his wife into making long buns to wrap the sausage with and "Voila" the birth of the all-American favorite, the Hot Dog!

CARAMEL POPCORN

8 or 9 cups popped corn
2 cups brown sugar
1 cup butter
1 tsp. salt
1½ cup white corn syryp
1 tsp. vanilla
½ tsp. soda

Boil all ingredients except soda for 5 minutes. Stir frequently.

Remove from heat and add baking soda.

Stir quickly and pour over popcorn, mixing well. Put into two large flat pans.

Bake at 250° for 1 hour, stirring often.

It was a great day for a race! The Great Mississippi Steamboat Race of 1870—when the Robert E. Lee won over the Natchez,

BUCKEYES

1½ cup creamy peanut butter
½ cup lightly salted butter or margarine, at room temperature
1 tsp. vanilla
1 16 oz. package confectioners sugar
1 6 oz. package semi sweet chocolate pieces
2 tbsp. solid vegetable shortening

Line a baking sheet with wax paper. In a medium size bowl mix peanut butter, butter, vanilla and sugar with hands to form a smooth dough. Mixture will be very stiff.

Shape dough into balls, using 2 tsp. for each. Place on wax paper and put in refrigerator.

In the top of a double boiler over simmering not boiling water, melt chocolate and shortening together. When smooth, pour into a small bowl or measuring cup.

Remove peanut butter balls from refrigerator. Insert a wooden toothpick into a ball and dip into melted chocolate so that ¾ of ball is coated. Return to wax paper and remove pick.

Repeat with all balls. Refrigerate on wax paper 30 minutes or longer, until chocolate is firm not sticky.

To store, remove balls from wax paper and place in plastic container with wax paper between layers to keep separate.

Carthage, Missouri, on the western border of the state, lies at the edge of the great western plains. It is a beautiful city, known worldwide for its beautiful marble. The marble is remarkable in color and durability and is used in the Missouri State Capital.

JOLLY BOURBON BALLS

½ cup finely chopped nuts
½ cup finely chopped candied cherries
½ cup bourbon
1 stick butter
1-1 lb. box confectioner's sugar
2-8 oz. boxes semi-sweet chocolate
1 box paraffin

Combine nuts and cherries in a bowl and stir in bourbon. Let stand 2 to 3 hours, drain well. Cream butter & sugar in bowl & add nuts & cherries. Shape in small balls & refrigerate for 30 mintues. Melt chocolate & paraffin in the top of a double boiler over hot water. Dip bourbon balls in melted chocolate mixture and place on waxed paper. Cool. Yield: 2 doz.

Jolly Mill, located in Southwest Missouri, in times past, was both a grain mill and a distillery. During the Civil War, the town around the mill was destroyed, but the bushwackers spared the mill. This was probably due to what was produced there, and it wasn't the flour! The town that grew up around the mill was called Jollification, a direct result of the product of the mill. Later they shortened the name to Jolly and it is said that the folks down there are still happy and always make these Bourbon Balls at Christmas.

SURVIVAL MUNCHIE STUFF

½ lb. chocolate chips
½ lb. M & Ms
½ lb. salted nuts (peanuts, cashews, walnuts, etc.)
¼ lb. shelled sunflower seeds
½ lb. chopped dried fruit (dates, raisins, apples or any combination)
2 cups dry cereal—any kind but flakes

Mix well and place in covered container.

This is great for bikers and campers or after school snacks.

The largest earthquake to ever shake the United States was not the famous San Francisco quake, but the New Madrid earthquake of 1811. It was so violent that the course of the Mississippi was said to flow north rather than south!

MISSOURI HERITAGE QUILT DESIGN — LOVE APPLE AND ROSE
MAKER: LAURA E. LYNES 1854–1921

This section taken from a quilt entitled "Love Apple and Rose" was created with extraordinary care. Paper patterns were used in the planning and design of this delicate and lacy-looking quilt.

Pickles, Preserves and Potions

WATERMELON RIND PICKLES

6 **pounds or ½ large watermelon rind, unpared**
¾ **cup salt**
3 **quarts of water**
2 **quarts (2 trays) ice cubes**
8 **cups sugar**
3 **cups white vinegar**
3 **cups water**
1 **tbsp. whole cloves**
6 **1-inch pieces stick cinnamon**
1 **lemon, thinly sliced, with
seeds removed**

Yield: 4 to 5 pints

Pare rind and all pink edges from the watermelon. Cut into 1 inch squares or fancy shapes as desired. Cover with brine made by mixing salt with 3 quarts cold water. Add ice cubes. Let stand 5 or 6 hours.

Drain and rinse with cold water. Cover with cold water and cook until fork-tender, about 10 minutes. *Do not overcook!* Drain.

Combine sugar, vinegar and water. Tie spices in a clean, thin, white cloth (cheesecloth) and add to pickling liquid. Boil 5 minutes and pour over watermelon with spices; add lemon slices. Cover and let stand overnight in refrigerator.

Heat watermelon in syrup to boiling and cook until watermelon is translucent, about 10 minutes. Remove spice bag.

Sterilize jars. Pack hot pickles loosely into clean, hot pint jars. To each jar add one piece of stick cinnamon from spice bag. Cover with boiling syrup to within ½ inch of top. Remove air bubbles, wipe jar rims and adjust jar lids.

Process in boiling bath for 5 minutes. Begin timing when jars are placed in the boiling water.

Remove jars and place upright, several inches apart, on a wire rack to cool.

REFRIGERATOR PICKLES

Clean and sterilize jars. Slice cucumbers in jars and add sliced onion as you fill the jars (bottom, middle and top). Pack down as much as possible, pour the following uncooked syrup over the cucumbers:

4 cups sugar
4 cups white vinegar
½ cup noniodized salt
1⅓ tsp. tumeric
1⅓ tsp. celery seed
1⅓ tsp. mustard seed

Mix well until sugar is dissolved. Pour over pickles, put on lids and let set in refrigerator for 5 days before using. They will keep one year in the refrigerator.

Big Spring, near Van Buren, Missouri is the largest single outlet spring in the United States. In an average day, the flow is 276 million gallons or the equivalent of about 500 good city water wells. The temperature of the water is a constant 55° and is part of the nation's first National Scenic Riverway. Early settlers used the cold water as a primitive form of refrigeration.

PICKLED PEACHES

8 pounds peeled peaches
(small to medium sizes)
6 cups sugar
4 sticks cinnamon (2 inches
long)
2 tbsp. whole cloves, crushed
1 tbsp. ginger
1 quart vinegar

Wash and peel peaches with a sharp knife, and drop into a cold solution of ½ tsp. ascorbic acid and 2 quarts water.

Place vinegar in a saucepan, add sugar, stir until dissolved. Cook over medium heat. Boil 5 minutes and skim off foam. Tie spices together in a clean, thin, white cloth (cheesecloth) and add to pickling liquid.

Drain peaches and place in boiling syrup. Cook until peaches can be pierced with a fork, but are not soft. Remove from heat, cover and allow peaches to set in syrup overnight in refrigerator to plump.

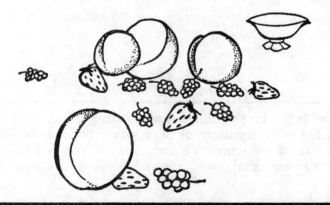

GRANDMA'S OLD FASHIONED PICKLED BEETS

3 quarts whole small beets
1 tbsp. whole allspice
2 cinnamon sticks
2 cups sugar
1½ tsp. salt
3½ cups vinegar
1½ cups water

Wash beets. Trim, leaving 2-inch stems and taproots. Cover with boiling water and cook whole until tender. Drain, peel and slice.

Loosely tie allspice and cinnamon sticks in a clean, thin, white cloth (cheesecloth). Combine sugar, salt, vinegar and water and add spice bag. Bring syrup to boil; simmer for 15 minutes. Remove spice bag.

Pack hot beets into hot pint jars. Cover with hot syrup to within ½ inch of top. Remove air bubbles, wipe jar rims and adjust jar lids.

Process in a boiling-water bath for 30 minutes. Begin timing when jars are placed in boiling water.

Remove jars and place upright, several inches apart, on a wire rack to cool.

Yield 6 pints.

CORN RELISH

1 doz. ears of corn
1 doz. green peppers
3 red peppers
4 cups onion, minced
2 qt. vinegar
1 qt. sugar
2 qts. ripe tomatoes, chopped
1 cup cucumber, peeled, seeded and chopped
½ cup salt
2 tbsp. celery seed
2 tbsp. mustard seed
2 tsp. tumeric seed

Chop all ingredients. Mix together with fresh corn cut from the cobs.

Cook to boil and let boil for 40 minutes until slightly thickened.

Seal relish in sterilized Mason jars while hot. Process in boiling water bath for 15 min.

From the years 1838 to 1849, Missouri and Iowa fought over disputed land on the northern boundary of Missouri. There was a so-called "Honey War;" over ownership of bee trees. An almost funny situation presented itself when a Missouri sheriff was arrrested in Iowa, the arresting officer indicted in Missouri and yet a second Missouri officer arrested in Iowa. The United States Supreme Court finally stepped in and settled the entire affair by dividing up the disputed land equally between the two states.

WILD GAME MARINADE

1 lg. onion, sliced
3 carrots, sliced
4 green onions, chopped (both bulbs and stems)
1 bay leaf
10 black peppercorns (crushed)
6 juniper berries (crushed)
6 whole cloves
1 small bunch parsley, chopped
¼ tsp. thyme
1 clove garlic, crushed
¼ tsp. rosemary
1 cup red wine
1 cup peanut oil
¼ cup wine vinegar
1 tsp. salt
1 tbsp. sugar

Mix all ingredients very well. Marinate meat for at least 24 hours or up to 3 days. Drain meat and cook as desired. Some of the marinade may be strained and used with pan drippings for gravy.

The area around Augusta, Missouri was the first in the United States to be recognized as a distinct viticultural region. Little Augusta, Mo. is the nation's first distinct wine district. Augusta wines won gold medals at the Chicago World's Fair in 1893 and also at the 1904 World's Fair in S. Louis.

Use some good Missouri wine in this recipe for Wild Game Marinade.

CORNCOB JELLY

10 corn cobs (cleaned of kernels)
5 cups water
1 tsp. cider vinegar
1 tbsp. powdered pectin
3 cups sugar
yellow food coloring

Boil corncobs in water until there is about 3 cups of corn "juice". Strain and add vinegar, pectin and sugar. Return to heat and stir constantly. Simmer until sugar dissolves, then return to boil and cook for seven minutes. Add a drop or two of food coloring and pour into sterilized jars. Seal with melted paraffin.

Franklin County, Mo. is today the only place in the world where corncob pipes are produced. The little town of Washington, Mo. is known as the "Corncob Pipe Capitol of the World". Accomplished pipe smokers appreciate corncob pipes for their unique "cool smoke".

If you are not a pipe smoker you might want to try making some corncob jelly instead.

ORANGE LEMONADE

10 oranges, cut and squeezed
6 lemons, cut and squeezed
1½ cups sugar
   enough water and ice to
   make ½ gallon.

This refreshing summer drink will be a favorite with kids and grownups alike.

Squeeze oranges and lemons into pitcher. Add sugar and stir to dissolve. Add water and ice and stir. Taste and add more sugar if necessary.

ORANGE

Every year in August, the Missouri State Fair is held in Sedalia. Exhibits, displays and performers draw 300,000 visitors, including wide-eyed children who see, for the first time, farm animals and that all time favorite, the Missouri mule.

There are still old-time competitions for the best homemade preserves, or the biggest and best Missouri hog.

Everyone has a good time strolling the grounds and perhaps sipping some fresh home-made lemonade.

SASSAFRAS TEA
(To calm your nerves!)

1 young sassafras root, 2–3"
   long
1 qt. water

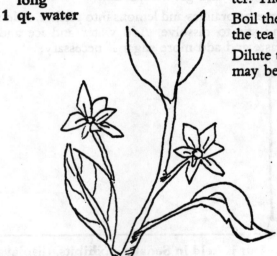

Scrub the root well with a brush under running water. Then peel off the outer "bark".

Boil the root in water for about 25 minutes or until the tea has a strong fragrance.

Dilute to suit your taste with boiling water. Sugar may be added as indicated.

Meramec Caverns, near Sullivan, Missouri is historically and geologically one of the states more interesting caverns. Jesse James and his gang used the caverns as a hideout until they were trailed there by a posse. The posse thought they had Jesse for sure, but after a three day gunfight Jesse and his gang escaped by following an underground river. This escape route was not found until 1940.

Index

Jazzy Potato p 117

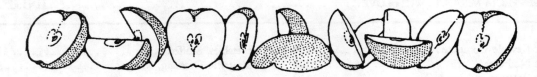

Additional copies of
Recipes From Missouri with Love
can be ordered for $9.95
from

THE BRANCHES
1389 Park Road
Chanhassen, MN 55317

Other cookbooks available from THE BRANCHES:
Recipes From Arizona With Love
Recipes From Iowa With Love
Recipes From Maine With Love
Recipes From Massachusetts With Love
Recipes From Minnesota With Love
Winning Recipes From Minnesota With Love
Winning Recipes From Wisconsin With Love
Winning Recipes From South Dakota With Love
The Just For Kids Cookbook
Chocolate Mousse Cookbook

All cookbooks are available for
$9.95 plus $1.95 shipping and handling.

Please make all checks payable to: **THE BRANCHES**

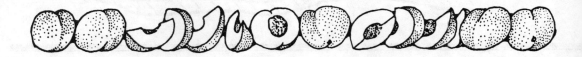